New English Lan

E L Black M A M Ed is the Principal
of Middleton St George College of Education and was
formerly Chief Examiner in English Language for the
Joint Matriculation Board and for the University Entrance
and School Examinations Council of the University of London

F E S Finn B A is the Head
of the English Department of Exmouth School

Title-page illustration
V E Day
L S Lowry

E L Black   F E S Finn

John
Murray

New English Language Test Papers

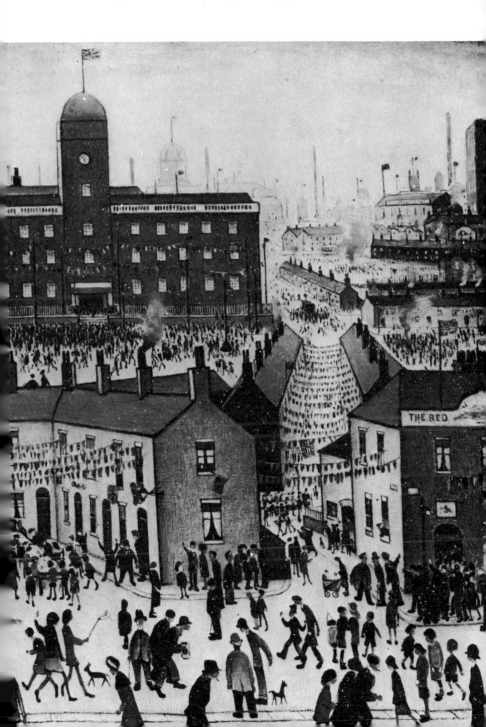

Printed Offset Litho in Great Britain by Cox and Wyman Ltd
London, Fakenham and Reading

0 7195 2070 3

Contents

Acknowledgments

The authors wish to record their thanks to the authors (or their agents or trustees) and publishers mentioned below the extracts for their permission to quote copyright material.

Thanks are also due to the following who have kindly permitted the reproduction of copyright illustrations:

Title-page ('V.E. Day' by L. S. Lowry), Glasgow Art Gallery and Museum; page 51 ('The Scream' by Edvard Munch), O. Vaering; page 52, British Broadcasting Corporation; page 76 (and front cover), Reproduced by permission of Punch; page 77, The Mansell Collection; page 121, South Wales Evening Post; page 122, Camera Press (Photographer Peter Mitchell); page 123, Edwin Smith.

Introduction

English Language papers at 'O' level are currently undergoing substantial changes. The general pattern remains unaltered: an essay question or questions, a passage on which summarizing questions are set, and an extract or extracts used to test comprehension. It is in the comprehension section of the papers that the biggest changes occur. Some boards are introducing multiple choice objective tests, as either compulsory or optional questions. This book contains test papers designed to give practice in essay writing, summarizing, and answering comprehension questions of the old and the new types.

Essay

All the papers contain essay titles of the free composition type; some of these questions require essays to be written about photographs. Some papers include a second group of essays which demand clear communication of information. A further list of titles is included at the end of the book to enable pupils to practise composition that involves writing a letter or a report, giving instructions, or writing short descriptions. One hour is usually allowed for the first type of essay, which should be about 450 words long, and about half an hour for the second.

Summary

All the papers contain passages for summarizing. Candidates are asked to summarize in whole or in part, and, in the longer extracts especially, to select relevant and reject irrelevant material.

Comprehension

To provide for an easy transition from the traditional type of comprehension question to the new multiple choice test, most of the comprehension exercises contain both kinds of questions. The traditional type of comprehension question needs no explanation, but the multiple choice objective test requires some introduction. Objective questions in this book consist of a stem with five responses, only one of which is correct. Obviously the marking of such tests presents no difficulty; a key is provided for the use of the teacher or pupil as desired. The questions in this book have been tried out on a large number of 'guinea-pigs'—pupils from the north and south of the country, boys and girls, able and less able pupils—in fact as varied a group of candidates as was necessary to ensure that these tests provided suitable practice.

Also included in this book are tables of statistics requiring interpretation by the pupil, a type of question which is sometimes included in the summary or comprehension section of Language papers.

Most examining boards allow one to one-and-a-half hours for the essay section (50% of the total marks) and two hours for the summary and comprehension (which account respectively for 15%–20% and 35%–30% of the total marks).

Paper 1

1 Write a composition on *one* of the following subjects:

   a Ideas for constructive or active or creative holidays.

   b Is censorship ever justified?

   c Choose a threat to our present life, such as the intensification of noise or the disfigurement of the countryside, and discuss measures to remove or lessen this threat.

   d Choose one way of making a living (e.g. farming) and show how much it has changed in recent years.

   e My most exciting experience.

   f 'Then the whining schoolboy, with his satchel
And shining morning face, creeping like snail
Unwillingly to school.'
Shakespeare wrote these lines in *As You Like It*. To what extent are they true today?

   g 'In pools beyond the reach of tide
The Senior Service cartons glide,
And on the sand the surf line lisps
With wrappings of potato crisps;
The beaches bring, with merry noise,
Tribute of broken plastic toys.'
Write on the problem suggested by these lines.

2 *Either*

   a Choose *one* of the following alternatives and state why you would prefer it to the other:
a motor cycle or a scooter; a holiday under canvas or a holiday in a caravan; reading a spy story or a detective story; playing a guitar or a violin.

Or

   b Write a letter to your local council asking for a useful alteration in your area or asking for provision of some service or facility that your area lacks. Invent suitable names and addresses.

Part Two
[*Time allowed: 1 hour*]

Read the following article and then answer the questions.

'Britain's best export,' I was told by the head of the Department
of Immigration in Canberra, 'is people.' Close on 100 000 people
have applied for assisted passages in the first five months of this
year, and half of these are eventually expected to migrate to
Australia.   5
    The Australians are delighted. They are keenly aware that
without a strong flow of immigrants into the workforce the
development of the Australian economy is unlikely to proceed at
the ambitious pace currently envisaged. The new mineral
discoveries promise a splendid future, and the injection of huge 10
amounts of American and British capital should help to ensure
that they are properly exploited, but with unemployment in
Australia down to less than 1·3 per cent, the government is
understandably anxious to attract more skilled labour.
    Australia is roughly the same size as the continental United 15
States, but has only twelve million inhabitants. Migration has
accounted for half the population increase in the last four years,
and has contributed greatly to the country's impressive economic
development. Britain has always been the principal source—
ninety per cent of Australians are of British descent, and Britain 20
has provided one million migrants since the Second World War.
    Australia has also given great attention to recruiting people
elsewhere. Australians decided they had an excellent potential
source of applicants among the so-called 'guest workers' who
have crossed their own frontiers to work in other parts of Europe. 25
There were estimated to be more than four million of them, and
a large number were offered subsidized passages and guaranteed
jobs in Australia. Italy has for some years been the second
biggest source of migrants, and the Australians have also
managed to attract a large number of Greeks and Germans.   30
    One drawback with them, so far as the Australians are con-
cerned, is that integration tends to be more difficult. Unlike the
British, continental migrants have to struggle with an unfamiliar language and new customs. Many naturally gravitate
towards the Italian or Greek communities which have grown up 35
in cities such as Sydney and Melbourne. These colonies have
their own newspapers, their own shops, and their own clubs. Their
inhabitants are not Australians, but Europeans.

The government's avowed aim, however, is to maintain 'a substantially homogeneous society into which newcomers, from 40 whatever sources, will merge themselves'. By and large, therefore, Australia still prefers British migrants, and tends to be rather less selective in their case than it is with others.

A far bigger cause of concern than the growth of national groups, however, is the increasing number of migrants who 45 return to their countries of origin. One reason is that people nowadays tend to be more mobile, and that it is easier than in the past to save the return fare, but economic conditions also have something to do with it. A slower rate of growth invariably produces discontent—and if this coincides with greater prosperity 50 in Europe, a lot of people tend to feel that perhaps they were wrong to come here after all.

Several surveys have been conducted recently into the reasons why people go home. One noted that 'flies, dirt, and outside lavatories' were on the list of complaints from British immigrants, 55 and added that many people also complained about 'the crudity, bad manners, and unfriendliness of the Australians'. Another survey gave climate conditions, homesickness, and 'the stark appearance of the Australian countryside' as the main reasons for leaving. 60

Most British migrants miss council housing, the National Health scheme, and their relatives and former neighbours. Loneliness is a big factor, especially among housewives. The men soon make new friends at work, but wives tend to find it much harder to get used to a different way of life. Many are 65 housebound because of inadequate public transport in most outlying suburbs, and regular correspondence with their old friends at home only serves to increase their discontent. One housewife was quoted recently as saying: 'I even find I miss the people I used to hate at home.' 70

Rents are high, and there are long waiting lists for Housing Commission homes. Sickness can be an expensive business and the climate can be unexpectedly rough. The gap between Australian and British wage packets is no longer big, and people are generally expected to work harder here than they do at home. 75 Professional men over forty often have difficulty in finding a decent job. Above all, perhaps, skilled immigrants often find a considerable reluctance to accept their qualifications.

According to the journal *Australian Manufacturer* the attitude of many employers and fellow workers is anything but friendly. 80

'We Australians,' it stated in a recent issue, 'are just too fond of painting the rosy picture of the big, warm-hearted Aussie. As a matter of fact, we are so busy blowing our own trumpets that we have not got time to be warm-hearted and considerate. Go down "heart-break alley" among some of the migrants and find out 85 just how expansive the Aussie is to his immigrants.'

WILLIAM DAVIS, 'Australia' (The Guardian)

After reading each of the following questions, choose the ONE correct answer, and indicate it by writing down the letter that stands for it. In all questions only ONE answer is correct. This is stressed in some questions but remember that the rule applies to all of them.

1 The Australians want a strong flow of immigrants because in Australia

  A immigrants speed up economic expansion
  B immigrants attract American and British capital
  C unemployment is down to a low figure
  D the government wants to maintain a substantially homogeneous society
  E Australia is as large as the United States

2 Australia prefers immigrants from Britain rather than from other countries because they are

  A like the 'guest workers' who cross European frontiers
  B more easily made part of local communities
  C selected carefully before entry
  D less likely to return home
  E less keen to live in large towns

3 This article stresses all the following reasons why British immigrants return to Britain with the ONE EXCEPTION of the

  A lack of subtle variations in Australian scenery
  B lack of friendliness among Australian people
  C lack of a National Health scheme
  D remoteness of their parents at home
  E tendency of Australia to resemble and copy America

4 'Currently' (l. 9) means

  A periodically
  B at present
  C following
  D generally accepted
  E optimistically

5 'Envisaged' (l. 9) means

  A imagined and hoped for

   B planned and contrived
   C estimated and assessed
   D expected and taken for granted
   E guaranteed and assumed

6 'Exploited' (l. 12) means

   A taken advantage of
   B financed
   C developed
   D exhausted
   E managed

7 'Accounted for' (l. 17) means

   A estimated
   B explained
   C been responsible for
   D reckoned
   E made possible

8 The two words in the second paragraph (ll. 6–14) that show that the writer is just a little unsure of Australia's future prosperity are

   A 'Australians' . . . . . . 'delighted'
   B 'keenly aware'
   C 'promise' . . . . . . 'should'
   D 'currently envisaged'
   E 'properly exploited'

9 'Gravitate towards' (l. 34) is nearest in meaning to

   A tend to
   B move to
   C like
   D join
   E are fascinated by

10 In explaining why some migrants return to Europe this article

   A stresses economic motives
   B emphasizes the variety of their motives
   C stresses loneliness and homesickness
   D stresses the difficulties of men over forty
   E gives most attention to the shortcomings of Australian social services

11 The last sentence (ll. 84–6) pictures the Australians as

   A spreading to the outback
   B unsympathetic
   C undemonstrative
   D ungenerous
   E narrow-minded

12 The word that is most clearly and obviously used as a metaphor is

   A 'expected' (l. 4)
   B 'exploited' (l. 12)
   C 'development' (l. 19)
   D 'pace' (l. 9)
   E 'attract' (l. 14)

13 In planning his material the writer tends, on the whole, to

   A give first the opinions of the Australians and then those of the immigrants
   B contradict in the second half of his article what he says in the first
   C cast indirect ridicule at the quotations he makes from various speakers
   D pass from generalization to supporting examples
   E stress first how men react, and then how women react

14 The conclusion to be drawn from the article is that the reasons why migrants return home are

   A very varied and difficult to prevent
   B not intensified by how individual Australians behave
   C largely economic
   D equally potent in periods of depression and prosperity
   E likely to affect men and women equally

15 The phrase 'integration tends to be more difficult' (l. 32) means that migrants from the continent of Europe find it harder to

   A learn Australian customs and interests
   B find suitable jobs in Australia
   C spread all over the Australian continent
   D form a balanced and mature personality
   E forget the national hatreds that they learnt in Europe

16 Which ONE of the following words is used literally, *not* metaphorically?

   A 'flow' (l. 7)
   B 'injection' (l. 10)
   C 'source' (l. 29)
   D 'recruiting' (l. 22)
   E 'selective' (l. 43)

17 All the following qualities are characteristic of the writer with the ONE EXCEPTION of his

   A use of humorous anecdote
   B interest in economics
   C love of picturesque exaggerations
   D resolve to see everyone's point of view
   E slight hostility towards Australians

18 'The growth of national groups' (l. 44) means the tendency of

   A British migrants to feel homesick

   B European migrants to mix *only* with fellow nationals

   C all migrants to develop into over-patriotic Australians

   D migrants from Europe to overpopulate a few areas

   E migrants to introduce into Australia feuds originating in Europe

19 Which ONE of the following topics does the article say most about?

   A farming in Australia

   B outdoor life on the beach

   C Australia's military problems

   D the homesickness of women immigrants

   E differences between the seven separate Australian states

20 Which of the following remarks about the article is *not* justified?

   A the first sentence is supposed to be both witty and true

   B each paragraph usually introduces a definitely different topic

   C the Australian government phrase that is quoted in ll. 39–41 is repeated a little ironically in order to suggest that it is optimistic propaganda

   D many of the quotations from what people say are intended to be ridiculous and uninformative

   E it treats sympathetically the immigrants' complaints about Australia

Additional Question
[*Time allowed: 50 minutes*]

21 Using your own words as far as possible, summarize what this passage says about:

   a Why Australia needs immigrants (40 words).

   b Why Australians prefer immigrants from Britain to those from elsewhere (40 words).

   c Why some migrants return home from Australia (100 words).

Paper 2

Part One

[*Time allowed: 1 hour for question 1 ; 30 minutes for question 2*]

1 Write a composition on *one* of the following subjects:

a An adventure on Dartmoor.
b Black magic.
c My earliest recollections.
d Symbols of the Seventies.
e Red herrings.
f Try to account for the increasing unrest and violence in our society. You might deal with race riots, disturbances at sporting events, strikes, and demonstrations.
g The countryside in winter.
h Why I should like to emigrate.

2 Describe carefully your feelings as you watched *one* of the following. You may use such descriptive detail of appearance, time, place etc. as you feel is necessary, but it is the impression formed of the person concerned which is important. Write about 25 lines.

a A woman sitting in the waiting-room before taking her driving test.
b A long-distance lorry driver taking a snack in a café.
c A teacher looking rather tired and harassed at the end of a day's work.
d An immigrant who is feeling the effects of our climate.
e A student whose dress and appearance are such as to excite comment.
f A batsman waiting in the pavilion before going in to bat.

Part Two

[*Time allowed: 1 hour*]

Read the following passage and then answer the questions.

A bus took him to the West End, where, among the crazy coloured fountains of illumination, shattering the blue dusk with green and crimson fire, he found the café of his choice, a tea-shop that had gone mad and turned Babylonian, a white palace with ten

thousand lights. It towered above the older buildings like a   5
citadel, which indeed it was, the outpost of a new age, perhaps a
new civilization, perhaps a new barbarism; and behind the thin
marble front were concrete and steel, just as behind the careless
profusion of luxury were millions of pence, balanced to the
last halfpenny. Somewhere in the background, hidden away,   10
behind the ten thousand lights and acres of white napery and
bewildering glittering rows of teapots, behind the thousand
waitresses and cash-box girls and black-coated floor managers
and temperamental long-haired violinists, behind the mounds of
shimmering bonbons and multi-coloured Viennese pastries, the   15
cauldrons of stewed steak, the vanloads of harlequin ices, were a
few men who went to work juggling with fractions of a farthing,
who knew how many units of electricity it took to finish a steak-
and-kidney pudding and how many minutes and seconds a
waitress (five feet four in height and in average health) would   20
need to carry a tray of given weight from the kitchen lift to the
table in the far corner. In short, there was a warm, sensuous,
vulgar life flowering in the upper storeys, and a cold science
working in the basement. Such was the gigantic tea-shop into
which Turgis marched, in search not of mere refreshment but of   25
all the enchantment of unfamiliar luxury. Perhaps he knew in his
heart that men have conquered half the known world, looted
whole kingdoms, and never arrived in such luxury. The place
was built for him.

It was built for a great many other people too, and, as usual,   30
they were all there. It steamed with humanity. The marble
entrance hall, piled dizzily with bonbons and cakes, was as
crowded and bustling as a railway station. The gloom and grime
of the streets, the raw air, all November, were at once left behind,
forgotten: the atmosphere inside was golden, tropical, belonging   35
to some high mid-summer of confectionery. Disdaining the lifts,
Turgis, once more excited by the sight, sound, and smell of it all,
climbed the wide staircase until he reached his favourite floor,
where an orchestra, led by a young Jewish violinist with wandering
lustrous eyes and a passion for tremolo effects, acted as a magnet   40
to a thousand girls. The door was swung open for him by a page;
there burst, like a sugary bomb, the clatter of cups, the shrill
chatter of white-and-vermilion girls, and, cleaving the golden,
scented air, the sensuous clamour of the strings; and, as he stood
hesitating a moment, half dazed, there came, bowing, a sleek   45
grave man, older than he was and far more distinguished than he

could ever hope to be, who murmured deferentially: 'For one, sir? This way, please.' Shyly, yet proudly, Turgis followed him.

J. B. PRIESTLEY, *Angel Pavement* (Heinemann)

After reading each of the following questions, choose the ONE correct answer, and indicate it by writing down the letter that stands for it. In all questions only ONE answer is correct. This is stressed in some questions, but remember that the rule applies to all of them.

1 The following words or phrases are somewhat critical of the tea-shop with the ONE EXCEPTION of

   A '. . . . . . . turned Babylonian' (l. 4)
   B 'perhaps a new barbarism' (l. 7)
   C 'acres of white napery' (l. 11)
   D 'juggling with fractions of a farthing' (l. 17)
   E 'balanced to the last halfpenny' (l. 9)

2 The following phrases or sentences are intended to be slightly ridiculous with the ONE EXCEPTION of

   A 'the crazy coloured fountains of illumination' (l. 1)
   B 'temperamental long-haired violinists' (l. 14)
   C 'five feet four in height and in average health' (l. 20)
   D 'it was built for a great many other people too' (l. 30)
   E 'the gloom and grime of the streets, the raw air, all November, were at once left behind' (l. 33)

3 That 'behind the thin marble front were concrete and steel' (ll. 7–8) suggests that

   A there was a fundamental falseness in the architecture and the appeal of the café
   B the tea-shop was based on physical foundations and an economic plan of real strength
   C the tea-shop failed to be as luxurious as Turgis hoped
   D the architect had made a sensible blend of old and new building materials
   E modern realistic commercialism existed behind the luxurious appearance

4 The following words *stress* the exotic nature of the West End and its obvious features with the ONE EXCEPTION of

   A 'crazy' (l. 1)
   B 'coloured' (l. 1)
   C 'crimson fire' (l. 3)
   D 'Babylonian' (l. 4)
   E 'a new civilization' (l. 7)

5 The author's sympathy with Turgis's desire to taste some luxury is shown by all the following words or phrases with the ONE EXCEPTION of

A 'the café of his choice' (l. 3)
B 'warm, sensuous, vulgar life' (l. 22)
C 'in search not of mere refreshment' (l. 25)
D 'it steamed with humanity' (l. 31)
E 'the atmosphere inside was golden' (l. 35)

6 The author's attitude to the café is

A fundamentally critical
B entirely critical
C slightly admiring
D completely neutral
E rather undecided

7 The marble front of the café was

A tasteful
B simple
C misleading
D luxurious
E artistic

8 A word in the second half of the first paragraph which the author uses to convey disapproval is

A 'warm' (l. 22)
B 'sensuous' (l. 22)
C 'vulgar' (l. 23)
D 'flowering' (l. 23)
E 'refreshment' (l. 25)

9 In its context the statement that 'the place was built for him' (ll. 28–9) really means that the café was intended to

A please simple people in a simple way
B exploit gullible people like him
C attract an exclusive clientele
D provide relaxation for tired young men
E satisfy a demand that already existed

10 Which ONE of the following statements about the second paragraph is *not* true?

A the café appealed to most senses simultaneously
B the café was both full of people and full of warmth
C the inside of the café contrasted with the weather outside
D this paragraph begins more bitterly than it ends
E this paragraph repeatedly stresses the commercial determination of the café owners

11 We deduce that Turgis was

   A rather poor
   B comparatively rich
   C extravagant
   D suspicious
   E hungry

12 'Deferentially' (l. 47) means

   A indifferently
   B exceptionally
   C respectfully
   D submissively
   E obsequiously

13 Which ONE of the following remarks about the punctuation is *not* true?

   A the comma after 'choice' (l. 3) could easily be replaced by a dash
   B if in the first paragraph this author has a list of words or phrases, he usually precedes the last one with a comma, unlike many writers
   C none of the semi-colons is used to emphasize a contrast
   D the comma in front of 'behind' (l. 34) does much the same work as 'and' would
   E the semi-colon after 'page' (l. 41) introduces a list

14 The author suggests that all the following adjectives (not in the text) could be applied to the owners of the shop with the ONE EXCEPTION of

   A mercenary
   B calculating
   C ostentatious
   D deceitful
   E cultured

15 The second paragraph does all the following with the ONE EXCEPTION of

   A providing a comic anticlimax after the preceding sentence
   B stressing how overcrowded the café was
   C ignoring the café's strong appeal to customers such as Turgis
   D resembling summer (in contrast to winter)
   E making the Jewish violinist seem appropriate to his surroundings

16 In the second paragraph all the following comparisons are made by the author's similes and metaphors with the ONE EXCEPTION that

   A the entrance hall is compared to a railway station (ll. 31–3)
   B the interior of the café is compared to warm countries (l. 35)
   C the violins are compared to people who shout (l. 44)
   D Turgis welcomed the lift like a conquering soldier gleefully accepting loot (l. 36)

E the darkness and dirt made the streets seem part of late autumn (ll. 33–4)

17 An *unsuitable* title for the passage would be

A Hidden persuasion
B A beautiful café
C Humble clerk and giant tea-shop
D Luxury for the many: profit for the few
E A cup of tea and a slice of glamour

18 Which ONE of the following words is used literally, *not* metaphorically?

A 'shattering' (l. 2)
B 'towered' (l. 5)
C 'outpost' (l. 6)
D 'citadel' (l. 6)
E 'juggling' (l. 17)

19 There is intended to be a deliberate contrast between the two halves of each of the following with the ONE EXCEPTION of

A 'mounds', 'cauldrons', 'vanloads' . . . . . . 'a few men' (ll. 14–17)
B 'warm, sensuous, vulgar life' . . . . . . 'cold science' (ll. 22–3)
C 'flowering in the upper storeys' . . . . . . 'working in the basement' (ll. 23–4)
D 'all November' . . . . . . 'high mid-summer' (ll. 34–6)
E 'wandering lustrous eyes' . . . . . . 'acted as a magnet' (ll. 39–40)

20 'Enchantment' (l. 26) means

A pleasure
B magic
C deception
D opulence
E thrill

Additional Question
[*Time allowed: 40 minutes*]

21 a Explain the features of the tea-shop that this novelist disapproves of, and show how he communicates his disapproval.
   b Explain the features of the tea-shop that he approves of, and show how he communicates his approval.
   c What analogy is made between the method of building the café and the method of organizing it?

Paper 3

1 Write a composition on *one* of the following subjects:

    a Write a description that ends—'I hope I shall never go there again'.

    b Describe two very different buildings that you have found interesting.

    c Explain the pleasures of some active hobby, e.g. sailing.

    d Discuss any plans you sympathize with for abolishing or reforming *either* some feature of school life such as examinations or uniforms, *or* some feature of the law such as statutes about Sunday Observance.

    e A local society has offered a prize for the best guide-book entry to describe your town or village. Write a mischievous entry that includes some inconvenient home-truths.

    f What seems to you worthwhile in some form of popular literature, e.g. spy stories, science fiction?

    g My friends' faults.

    h The blackness of winter.

2 *Either*

    a You are secretary of your school historical society. Write a letter to the custodian of a historical building asking at what hours it opens on a certain day, and asking for other relevant information, e.g. are charges reduced for large parties and are refreshments available? Invent suitable names and addresses.

  Or

    b Describe for a foreign visitor the place in British life of *one* of the following:

        Guy Fawkes Night; The Grand National; The Cup Final; Speech Day; Mothering Sunday; Pantomime.

Part Two

[*Time allowed: 1 hour*]

Read the following passage then answer the questions.

Laymen suspect that because colds are self-limiting, short, non-fatal infections, doctors do not take them very seriously. Nobody will think this after reading Sir Christopher Andrewes's book.

An American survey has shown that each year every employed 5 person loses three to four working days from colds and allied complaints, and every school child loses five to six days of schooling. Colds waste more time than strikes. The conquest of the common cold is therefore a thoroughly worthwhile ambition.

Until 1961 Sir Christopher Andrewes was in charge of the 10 Medical Research Council's Common Cold Research Unit at Salisbury, and he writes as one of the world's experts when he describes the patience, the frustrations, the ingenuity and occasional flashes of true scientific genius which have characterized the careers of the workers who have set out to tackle what has 15 turned out to be a real brute of a problem.

The great killing infections like syphilis or poliomyelitis are each caused by one specific micro-organism, or, at worst, a small group of closely related parasites. By contrast it has slowly become apparent that the common cold is not a disease but a 20 large group of similar diseases, caused, possibly, by anything between fifty and one hundred different organisms.

Much of Sir Christopher's book is taken up by an account of the struggle to identify the germs which do cause colds. At first it was thought that bacteria were responsible because certain 25 bacteria are commonly found in the noses and throats of cold victims. The first evidence that a virus might be concerned was obtained in 1914 when Dr. W. Kruse of the Hygienic Institute of the University of Leipzig took some of the discharge from the nose of an assistant with a cold in the head, diluted the discharge 30 in saline, and then passed it through a filter with pores too small to permit the passage of bacteria. Drops of the filtrate were put into the noses of twelve other members of the staff and four of them developed colds within a day or so.

Since that time thousands of volunteers have subjected them- 35 selves to similar experimental infections, and for nearly twenty years most of such work has been done at Salisbury where the

guinea pigs are rewarded by a ten-day holiday, all found . . .
This 'clumsy, expensive and unreliable' use of human volunteers
was necessary because for a long time chimpanzees were the only   40
other animals known to be susceptible to infection by common
cold germs, and chimpanzees were far too expensive and unruly
for routine use.

Growing cold viruses in the laboratory also proved difficult
until one of the men involved demonstrated his possession of that   45
most precious scientific faculty—serendipity.

Cold viruses were being grown with only moderate success in
laboratory cultures of lung tissue from human embryos. The lung
tissue cultures were kept alive by a salt solution containing added
vitamins and a number of other ingredients. One day at Salisbury   50
Dr. David Tyrrell found that this salt solution was faulty, and in
order to keep his tissue cultures going he hastily borrowed a
supply from another laboratory. When the imported solution
was added to tissue cultures infected with cold viruses the lung
tissue cells began to degenerate in a manner typical of tissues   55
parasitized by active viral particles.

Dr. Tyrrell soon discovered that the borrowed fluid provided a
more acid medium in his culture tubes than that produced by the
native Salisbury brew. The nose provides a slightly acid environment, and Dr. Tyrrell realized that a degree of acidity was just   60
what nose-inhabiting viruses needed in order to thrive outside
the body. Thus a happy accident enabled a perspicacious
scientist to modify the cold virus culture technique and thence
forward the whole exercise proved far easier and more profitable.

. . . Much of common cold folklore is demolished. Draughts,   65
chilling and wet feet do not bring colds on, says Sir Christopher,
and clean, healthy living with lots of fresh air, plenty of exercise,
good, plain food and a cold bath every morning may be good for
the soul and the waistline, but does nothing to keep cold viruses
at bay.   70

Colds are not very infectious (which will surprise most of us), so
there is really no excuse for staying away from work when you
have one. All the remedies so far invented have one thing in
common—they are useless. In temperate countries, colds are
commoner during the winter, but what the 'winter factor' is   75
which brings them on remains unknown. Most of us harbour
cold viruses in our noses throughout the year, and many colds are
probably not 'caught' at all, but start because somehow the
resident viruses become activated from time to time.

To write a book about colds at this stage, says Sir Christopher,   80
is rather like writing a review of a play in the middle of the first
act. Since he wrote those words, workers at Salisbury have
announced the production of the first cold vaccine which will
protect against infection by one particular cold virus. Unfortunately there are very many cold viruses and complete immunity   85
from colds by vaccination would require the administration of a
separate vaccine for every virus in the book.

DR. DONALD GOULD in New Scientist

1 Using your own words as far as possible, summarize what the passage
  says about:
  a Why it is important to prevent the common cold (about 40 words).
  b Why it is difficult to prevent or cure the common cold (about 100
    words).
  c The three most effective steps so far taken in research on the
    common cold (about 80 words).

2 Why does Sir Christopher say that 'to write a book about colds at this
  stage is rather like writing a review of a play in the middle of the first
  act'? Write four or five sentences.

Part Three

[*Time allowed: 45 minutes*]

After reading each of the following questions set on the passage in Part
Two, choose the ONE correct answer, and indicate it by writing down the
letter that stands for it. In all questions only ONE answer is correct. This is
stressed in some questions, but remember that the rule applies to all of
them:

1 The main reason why the common cold is difficult to deal with is that it
  A is more common in winter than in summer
  B wastes more time than strikes
  C is really fifty to one hundred different diseases
  D is not likely to attack many types of animal
  E is not due to draughts, chilling and wet feet

2 The prevention of all colds is
  A improbable
  B very difficult
  C impossible
  D imminent
  E dependent upon good health

3 One can deduce from the passage that colds are
- **A** not given enough attention by doctors
- **B** more frequent in America than in England
- **C** due to bacteria
- **D** likely to attack only very few types of animals
- **E** justifiable reasons for staying away from work

4 In the special context of l. 1 'laymen' means men who are not
- **A** priests
- **B** doctors
- **C** experts
- **D** specialists
- **E** scientists

5 To think colds unimportant is to think
- **A** superficially
- **B** obtusely
- **C** plausibly
- **D** inaccurately
- **E** sceptically

6 The first sentence (ll. 1–2) puts forward ideas that the writer later shows to be
- **A** important
- **B** out-of-date
- **C** unjustified
- **D** illustrative of a general point
- **E** illogical

7 'Ingenuity' (l. 13) means
- **A** initiative
- **B** skill
- **C** technique
- **D** commonsense
- **E** inventiveness

8 'Characterized' (l. 14) means
- **A** summed up
- **B** typified
- **C** distinguished
- **D** underlined
- **E** shaped

9 'Identify' (l. 24) means
- **A** recognize

B distinguish
C nullify
D study
E discover

10 'Routine' (l. 43) means

   A regular
   B frequent
   C continuous
   D controlled
   E accepted

11 'Serendipity' (l. 46) means the ability to make

   A valuable discoveries by logical thinking
   B unexpected discoveries by unusual foresight
   C logical discoveries by rational thinking
   D useful discoveries by building on earlier ones
   E happy discoveries by accident

12 'Thrive' (l. 61) means to become

   A prosperous
   B numerous
   C vigorous
   D erratic
   E infectious

13 The phrase 'a happy accident' (l. 62) means that Dr. Tyrrell's discovery was

   A likely to add to human happiness
   B paradoxical in that an accident made him happy
   C beneficial and unforeseen
   D lucky and due to coincidence
   E due to an unexpected event

14 The passage stresses that Dr. Tyrrell discovered how to

   A prevent colds in most circumstances
   B create colds artificially more effectively
   C prove that draughts and wet feet do not prevent colds
   D show that colds are not very infectious
   E immunize people against one particular virus

15 The passage assumes that colds present exactly the same problem in

   A Germany, America and Britain
   B hot and temperate climates
   C winter and summer
   D children and adults
   E very many different animals

16 The last sentence of the eleventh paragraph (ll. 76–9) is

   A proved
   B likely to be true
   C a mere theory
   D logically deduced
   E the subject of controversy

17 Which ONE of the following words is used literally, *not* metaphorically?

   A 'conquest' (l. 8)
   B 'struggle' (l. 24)
   C 'demolished' (l. 65)
   D 'useless' (l. 74)
   E 'harbour' (l. 76)

18 A word meaning *possessing a unique range of distinctive qualities* is

   A 'self-limiting' (l. 1)
   B 'allied' (l. 6)
   C 'specific' (l. 18)
   D 'certain' (l. 25)
   E 'susceptible' (l. 41)

Paper 4

Part One

[*Time allowed: 1 hour*]

Write a composition on *one* of the following subjects:

a 'History is little more than a register of the crimes, follies and misfortunes of mankind.'

b Write the opening chapter of a story (about 500 words). Make sure that your opening remarks are likely to interest your readers, and that the last sentences encourage him to turn to chapter 2.

c 'One law for the rich, another for the poor.' What truth is there in this saying?

d Why I should like to be a . . . .   Choose your occupation and say why it appeals to you.

e A ghost story.

f Crime and punishment. Give your views about the present system of probation, fines, detention centres, borstals and prisons. Should the punishment fit the crime?

g The newest member of the family.

h What help in running a home should a husband give to his wife?

Part Two

[*Time allowed: 1 hour*]

Read the following passage (which for your convenience has been divided into two sections) and then answer the questions.

[A] In 1952 you could meet the nineteenth century in the hotels and bars of Gibraltar, the furniture and décor long since discarded by England, tardily handed on to her colony. There was only one really first-class hotel, and it had the reputation—since improved—of high prices and low cuisine. The rest of the hotels   5 were of the transit type, designed for travelling salesmen, with a maximum of grim little sleeping-cells and a minimum of bathrooms and of public space. In one such paleotechnic hostelry Joan and I spent our first strange days in Gibraltar. Its Victorian wallpapers, gloomy oleographs, plastic flowers, tarnished gilt,   10

and ancient sanitation imposed a feeling of sadness, almost of
nostalgia. We had travelled far, not only in distance, we felt, but
in time as well.

Uneasily, among those dusty palms and aspidistras, we sensed
the environment of our great-grandparents—those definitely   15
pompous people who pose and glare beside their tragic wives in
yellowing daguerreotypes, those tyrants and tycoons of top
nation days, now mouldering hideously in carved coffins under
lush, lying epitaphs and hemispheres of waxen flowers . . .

I did not know then that much of this atmosphere drifts in-   20
exorably into Gibraltar from the overpowering land of Spain
which marches with it and influences it in many subtle ways.
There the horse-cab and oil-lamp, the chaperone and cuspidor,
the masher and the mistress, are still in their heyday, and gilded
furniture and crystal chandeliers are dashing innovations. Joan   25
and I felt, as most visitors must have felt, that these nostalgic
trappings, this oppressive Victoriana, were peculiarly Gibraltarian. You will still find strong traces of what I have described in
the hotels of Gibraltar, but happily a new generation of hoteliers'
sons, educated in England, has arrived and made much im-   30
provement, and most of the hotels have had, at least, their
faces lifted.

Whenever we could, Joan and I took refuge in the streets. The
Englishman's home is his castle because he has not much choice.
There is nowhere to sit in the streets of England, not even, after   35
twilight, in the public gardens. The climate, very often, does not
even permit him to walk abroad. Naturally, he stays indoors and
creates a cocoon of comfort. That was the way we lived in Belfast.

These southern people, on the other hand, look outwards. The
Spanish or Gibraltarian home is, typically, a small and crowded   40
apartment up several flights of dark and dirty stairs. In it, one,
two or even three old people share a few ill-lit rooms with the
young family. Once he has eaten, changed his clothes, embraced
his wife, kissed his children and his parents, there is nothing to
keep the southern man at home. He hurries out, taking even his   45
breakfast coffee at his local bar. He comes home late for his
afternoon meal after an aperitive hour at his café. He sleeps for
an hour, dresses, goes out again and stays out until late at night.
His wife does not miss him, for she is out, too—at the market in
the morning and in the afternoon sitting with other mothers,   50
baby-minding in the sun.

The usual Spanish or Gibraltarian home has no sitting-room,

living-room or lounge. The parlour of our working-class houses
would be an intolerable waste of space. Easy-chairs, sofas, divans
and such-like furniture are unknown. There are no bookshelves,   55
because there are no books. Talking and drinking, as well as
eating, are done on hard chairs round the dining-table, between
a sideboard embellished with the best glasses and an inevitable
display cabinet full of family treasures, photographs and
souvenirs. The elaborate chandelier over this table and, in Spain,   60
the rudimentary heating-stove beneath it proclaim it as the hasp
and hub of the household and of the family. 'Hearth and home'
makes no sense in the south of Spain, and very little in Gibraltar.
One's home is one's town or village, and one's hearth is the
sunshine.   65

Our northern towns are dormitories with cubicles, by comparison. When we congregate—in the churches it used to be, now in
the cinema, say, impersonally, or at public meetings, formally—
we are scarcely ever man to man. Only in our pubs can you find
the truly gregarious and communal spirit surviving, and in   70
England even the pubs are divided along class lines.

Along this Mediterranean coast, home is only a refuge and a
retreat. The people live together in the open air—in the street,
forum, *agora*, *plaza*, *piazza*, market-place. Down here, there is a
far stronger feeling of community than we had ever known. In   75
crowded and circumscribed Gibraltar, with its complicated
inter-marriages, its identity of interests, its surviving sense of
siege, one can see and feel an integrated society.

To live in a tiny town with all the organization and panoply of
a state, with Viceroy, Premier, Parliament, Press and Pentagon,   80
all in miniature, all within arm's reach, is an intensive course in
civics. In such an environment, nothing can be hidden, for better
or for worse. One's successes are seen and recognized; one's
failures are immediately exposed. Social consciousness is at its
strongest, with the result that there is a constant and firm pressure   85
towards good social behaviour, towards courtesy and kindness.
Gibraltar, with all its faults, is the friendliest and most tolerant of
places. Straight from the cynical anonymity of a big city, we
luxuriated in its happy personalism. We look back on it, like all
its exiled sons and daughters, with true affection.   90

[B] One step outside the grim portals of our hotel and the bright
sunshine dispelled our gloom and filled us with warmth and
optimism. This sun, which has made the Mediterranean shore a

cradle for so many civilizations, what does it really mean to man? Warmth, of course, which permits free social intercourse and which, by minimizing the work of building and the burden of tilling, allows more time for leisure and learning. But there is another quality, with less tangible results—the intensity of light.

Gibraltar is heavily tilted to the west and hangs over its bay, so that the afternoon light comes to it at double strength, directly from the sky and reflected from the water. Photographers doubt their exposure meters here, and stop down their lenses as never before. Architects scratch their heads at the tiny windows which can light large rooms. Sunglasses are the rule, rather than the exception.

The more light, the more colour. A grey stone in the sun here reminds you that grey is a mixture of colours. The light will find in it tints which we pay painters to find for us. Strong colours shriek in Gibraltar and even the drabbest deliver subtle, unexpected shades.

The southern people accept this gift of light, and live up to it. The women wear brighter clothes and hang bright curtains. Men paint their houses white or brilliant blue. Sober merchants buy vermilion motor-cars. Everyone rises to the occasion and pays his homage to the sun.

The people of Gibraltar take their sun for granted, and even decry it, at times, as a despoiler of feminine beauty and of infant health. They kept telling us not to trust it—it only *felt* hot, it was still cold. Do not change into cotton until May; never bathe before June. The weather may deceive, the calendar never.

But we, straight from our dark north, embraced the sun and its culture without restraint or suspicion. Perhaps this late gift should always have been ours, I reflected, for the earliest Irish people are said to have come up from the Mediterranean, and the Celts fought their way right down through Portugal to the southern coast.

The sun alone, that unbuyable boon, kept us in Gibraltar through thin times, as it keeps the hungry peasants lingering still in Calabria and Andalusia. The sun, that is to say, and the community culture which it fosters. Over the years, many emigrant Gibraltarians have left opportunities of wealth behind them in Britain or America and returned to The Rock, to low wages, overcrowding and, in the past, second-class citizenship. There are many reasons for their return, but the strongest are the pulls of place and race, the mild and constant joy of living in community with one's own people, the rare ease of social relationships here, and the sun which forms and warms it all.

JOHN D. STEWART, Gibraltar the Keystone (John Murray)

From Section A

'He (the Englishman) stays indoors . . . .' (l. 37)
'These southern people . . . . look outwards.' (l. 39)
Show how and why life and living conditions differ in England and Gibraltar. Use between 130 and 150 of your own words.

From Section B

'This sun, ... , what does it really mean to man?' (ll. 3–4)
Show how the Mediterranean sun affects the life of the Gibraltarian. Use about 50 of your own words.

Part Three

[Time allowed: 1 hour]

Read the following passage (which for your convenience has been divided into three sections) and then answer the questions.

[A] The fundamental characteristic of a guerrilla band is mobility. This permits it in a few minutes to move far from a specific theatre and in a few hours far even from the region, if that becomes necessary; permits it constantly to change front and avoid any type of encirclement. As the circumstances of the war   5
require, the guerrilla band can dedicate itself exclusively to fleeing from an encirclement which is the enemy's only way of forcing the band into a decisive fight that could be unfavourable; it can also change the battle into a counter-encirclement (small bands of men are presumably surrounded by the enemy when suddenly   10
the enemy is surrounded by stronger contingents; or men located in a safe place serve as a lure, leading to the encirclement and annihilation of the entire troops and supply of an attacking force). Characteristic of this war of mobility is the so-called minuet, named from the analogy with the dance: the guerrilla   15
bands encircle an enemy position, an advancing column for example; they encircle it completely from the four points of the compass, with five or six men in each place, far enough away to avoid being encircled themselves; the fight is started at any one of the points, and the army moves towards it; the guerrilla band then   20
retreats, always maintaining visual contact, and initiates its attack from another point. The army will repeat its action and the

guerrilla band the same. Thus, successively, it is possible to keep an enemy column immobilized, forcing it to expend large quantities of ammunition and weakening the morale of its troops   25
without incurring great dangers.

This same tactic can be applied at night time, closing in more and showing greater aggressiveness, because in these conditions counter-encirclement is much more difficult. Movement by night is another important characteristic of the guerrilla band, enabling   30
it to advance into position for an attack and, where the danger of betrayal exists, to mobilize in new territory. The numerical inferiority of the guerrilla makes it necessary that attacks always be carried out by surprise; this great advantage is what permits the guerrilla fighter to inflict losses on the enemy without suffering   35
losses. In a fight between a hundred men on one side and ten on the other, losses are not equal where there is one casualty on each side. The enemy loss is always reparable; it amounts to only one per cent of his effectives. The loss of the guerrilla band requires more time to be repaired because it involves a soldier of high   40
specialization and is ten per cent of the operating forces.

[B] Another fundamental characteristic of the guerrilla soldier is his flexibility, his ability to adapt himself to all circumstances, and to convert to his service all of the accidents of the action. Against the rigidity of classical methods of fighting, the guerrilla fighter invents his own tactics at every minute of the fight and constantly   5
surprises the enemy.

In the first place, there are only elastic positions, specific places the enemy cannot pass, and places of diverting him. Frequently the enemy, after easily overcoming difficulties in a gradual advance, is surprised to find himself suddenly and   10
solidly detained without possibilities of moving forward. This is due to the fact that the guerrilla-defended positions, when they have been selected on the basis of a careful study of the ground, are invulnerable. It is not the number of attacking soldiers that counts, but the number of defending soldiers. Once that number   15
has been placed there, it can nearly always hold off a battalion with success. It is a major task of the chiefs to choose well the moment and the place for defending a position without retreat.

.The form of attack of a guerrilla army is also different; starting with surprise and fury, irresistible, it suddenly converts itself into   20
total passivity. The surviving enemy, resting, believes that the attacker has departed; he begins to relax, to return to the routine

life of the camp or of the fortress, when suddenly a new attack bursts forth in another place, with the same characteristics, while the main body of the guerrilla band lies in wait to intercept 25 reinforcements. At other times an outpost defending the camp will be suddenly attacked by the guerrilla, dominated and captured. The fundamental thing is surprise and rapidity of attack.

[C] Acts of sabotage are very important. It is necessary to distinguish clearly between sabotage, a revolutionary and highly effective method of warfare, and terrorism, a measure that is generally ineffective and indiscriminate in its results, since it often makes victims of innocent people and destroys a large 5 number of lives that would be valuable to the revolution. Terror- ism should be considered a valuable tactic when it is used to put to death some noted leader of the oppressing forces well known for his cruelty, his efficiency in repression, or any other quality that makes his elimination useful. But the killing of persons of 10 small importance is never advisable, since it brings on an increase of reprisals, including deaths.

There is one point very much in controversy in opinions about terrorism. Many consider that its use, by provoking police oppression, hinders all more or less legal or semi-clandestine 15 contact with the masses and makes impossible unification for actions that will be necessary at a critical moment. This is correct; but it also happens that in a civil war the repression by the governmental power in certain towns is already so great that, in fact, every type of legal action is suppressed already, and any 20 action of the masses that is not supported by arms is impossible. It is therefore necessary to be circumspect in adopting methods of this type and to consider the consequences that they may bring for the revolution. At any rate, well-managed sabotage is always a very effective arm, though it should not be employed to put means 25 of production out of action, leaving a sector of the population paralysed (and thus without work) unless this paralysis affects the normal life of the society. It is ridiculous to carry out sabotage against a soft drink factory, but it is absolutely correct and advisable to carry out sabotage against a power plant. In the first 30 case, a certain number of workers are put out of a job but nothing is done to modify the rhythm of industrial life; but this is entirely justified by the paralysis of the life of the region.

CHE GUEVARA, *Guerrilla Warfare* (Monthly Review Press)

After reading each of the following questions, choose the ONE correct answer, and indicate it by writing down the letter that stands for it. In all questions only ONE answer is correct. This is stressed in some questions, but remember that the rule applies to all of them.

From Section A

1 'Theatre' (l. 3) means

   A building
   B scene of operations
   C battlefield
   D amphitheatre
   E district

2 'Contingents' (l. 11) means

   A additional forces
   B supply trains
   C experienced bodies of troops
   D parts of a large force
   E forces of infantry

3 'Lure' (l. 12) means

   A attraction
   B temptation
   C magnet
   D decoy
   E fascination

4 'Analogy with' (l. 15) means

   A agreement with
   B imitation of
   C discrepancy from
   D similarity to
   E suitability to

5 'Maintaining visual contact' (l. 21) means

   A looking for trouble
   B keeping in sight
   C watching closely
   D keeping good discipline
   E sending out scouts

6 'Aggressiveness' (l. 28) means

   A strength of purpose

B threatening behaviour
C eagerness to take the offensive
D quarrelsomeness
E anger

7 Guerrillas must always make surprise attacks; which ONE of the following is *not* a true reason for this?
A they are fewer in number than the enemy
B they can afford to incur casualties
C they can inflict losses without sustaining any
D casualties are more serious to guerrillas than to regular troops
E they are more mobile than regular troops

8 The author is very optimistic about what guerrillas can achieve. The following phrases all illustrate his optimism with the ONE EXCEPTION of
A 'in a few minutes to move' (l. 2)
B 'avoid any type of encirclement' (l. 5)
C 'change the battle into a counter-encirclement' (l. 9)
D 'this same tactic can be applied at night time' (l. 27)
E 'losses are not equal where there is one casualty on each side' (l. 37)

From Section B

9 'Accidents' (l. 3) means
A calamities
B slight mishaps
C unexpected events
D misfortunes
E irregular acts

10 'Rigidity' (l. 4) means
A cruel harshness
B bloody losses
C tactical sameness
D professional strictness
E traditional nobility

11 The author holds the optimistic view that guerrilla positions cannot be captured when they are
A defended by resolute soldiers
B attacked by small numbers of soldiers
C strengthened by fortifications
D placed on well-chosen sites
E defended by flexible forces

12 Suppose you do not believe anything in this extract. Which ONE of the following arguments would it *not* be fair to use against it?

    A the phrases 'elastic positions' and 'specific places that the enemy cannot pass' (ll. 7–8) seem to contradict one another

    B to stress the defence of 'a position without retreat' (l. 18) is to contradict the earlier emphasis on flexibility

    C especially in ll. 9–11 the author expects the impossible of guerrillas

    D it is rash to describe guerrillas' positions, or in fact anyone's, as 'invulnerable' (l. 14)

    E the author does not give sufficient emphasis to surprise

13 'Pass' (l. 8) means to

    A overwhelm
    B avoid
    C slip past
    D advance beyond
    E ignore

14 'Diverting him' (l. 8) means

    A attracting the enemy's amused disdain
    B persuading him to by-pass more important points
    C preventing him from overwhelming essential defences
    D resisting him successfully
    E persuading him to dissipate his forces

15 Which ONE of the following does the last paragraph (ll. 19–29) *not* advise the guerrillas to do?

    A start an action with a furious attack
    B later lull the enemy into a false sense of security
    C press home continuous attacks
    D divide itself into several groups
    E switch the point of its attack quickly

From Section C

16 'Indiscriminate' (l. 4) means

    A unfair
    B haphazard
    C accidental
    D unintentional
    E confused

17 Sabotage should be used to

    A terrorize the enemy
    B cause unemployment in most civilian industries
    C paralyse the life of a particular area

D kill as many people as possible
E destroy all factories

18 The author advocates terrorism when it

A kills people who would help a revolution to succeed
B can be used to kill a leading oppressor
C provokes reprisals
D incites stern action by the police
E never achieves the desired results

19 The author urges saboteurs to be

A ruthless
B selective
C discreet
D correct
E well advised

20 'Semi-clandestine' (l. 15) means half

A illegal
B revolutionary
C hidden
D secret
E underground

From the Whole Passage

21 Which ONE of the following is *not* an essential element of guerrilla tactics?

A ability to move freely
B friendship with local people
C knowledge of the ground
D complete numerical superiority
E knowledge of escape routes

22 Of all the paragraphs the last (ll. C. 13–33) is the least

A open in connecting guerrilla warfare with revolution
B interested in winning the sympathy of a majority of a nation
C aware that the police, as well as the army, will resist guerrillas
D dogmatic in being sure that one clear plan is always right
E critical of existing governments

Paper 5

Part One

[*Time allowed: 1 hour for question 1; 30 minutes for question 2*]

1 Write a composition on *one* of the following subjects:
   a Interesting neighbours.
   b Various forms of prejudice.
   c Imagine that you are an American, accustomed to baseball or American football, and describe the first game of cricket or association football that you see after arriving in England.
   d You are confined to your house or your bedroom or a hospital bed. You hear outside the noise of some activity (e.g. a fair or a football match) that you would like to join and cannot. Describe your feelings.
   e One of the happenings in a novel you have written is based upon a childhood event which much influenced you. Reproduce this part of your novel.
   f The wedding of one of the members of your family.
   g Pony-trekking.

2 *Either*
   a Write a letter to the press stating the case *either* for abolishing examinations *or* for handing over school discipline to a committee in which staff and students co-operate on equal terms. Invent suitable names and addresses.
   Or
   b Write a clear account of how to look after one type of animal.

Part Two

[*Time allowed: 1 hour*]

The passage below is about sheep-farming in North Wales. Read it carefully and then answer the questions, using your own words as far as possible.

The mountain farmer's year begins with the lambing season when he patrols his flock twice a day for about a month; acting as midwife in difficult cases; trying to persuade ewes who have lost

their lambs to suckle a motherless lamb or one of twin lambs;
taking sheep eighty miles to the nearest vet, if necessary; and   5
hoping, by the end of this time, to have eighty lambs: approx-
imately forty ewes and forty wethers, for each hundred of his
flock of ewes. Lambing begins early in April and shortly after-
wards the whole flock is sent up the mountain, the new arrivals
having been ear-marked and wool-marked with the sign and   10
mark of the farm to which they belong. Mountain farms may
either have a mountain or part of a mountain, fenced off, included
in their land, or rights to keep a certain number of sheep on an
open mountain. There is a prohibition on putting fences round
pieces of open mountain. When a number of farmers' flocks graze   15
an open mountain, the sheep know their own part of the mountain
and rear their lambs there. Because of this knowledge, called
'cynefin', these sheep have an extra value when sold to the next
tenant who comes into the farm. If new sheep were bought and
put on an open mountain they would have to be taught their   20
place. The shepherd would tie a front-foot to their necks and stay
up the mountain with them almost constantly until they knew
their place. This 'raising the knowledge' in the sheep ('codi
cynefin') was done in the past, when the mountains were under-
stocked because of deaths in the flocks or previous poverty,   25
and a farmer wished and was able to increase his flock quickly.
Nowadays, it is generally true to say that the farmers are grazing
as many sheep as they have grazing rights for; but should they
wish to increase their flock they would do so by selling fewer ewes
than usual. The sheep's knowledge of their part of the mountain is   30
a substitute for boundary fences and round-the-year shepherding
and so when mountain sheep are sold it is always to an incoming
tenant: they are not sold off the farm and their cynefin is sold with
them. If a sheep farmer kept too many sheep on the mountain he
shared with other farmers his sheep would suffer very badly before   35
his neighbours' suffered; because of the cynefin. His sheep,
although crowded and undernourished, would still keep very
largely to his part of the mountain. Nevertheless, in such circumstances, there would be some spread and if the over-stocking
farmer were a very large farmer and his neighbour were very   40
small, his neighbour could not stand a small loss so well as he
could stand a large loss. He could 'push his neighbour over' a
little, by making him reduce his flock first.

The flocks are sent up to the mountain in the spring and brought
down in the winter at a time agreed upon by all the farmers   45

concerned and fixed beforehand so that no one flock is longer on the mountain pasture than the others. During the summer the sheep are brought down to be shorn and dipped in insecticide. The new grass which grows on hayfields after the hay has been cut is called the 'aftermath' and in late summer the wether lambs are   50 brought down from the mountain and fed either on this rich 'aftermath' or on rape specially grown for the purpose. Fattened thus for a month or two, they are then sold, together with the oldest ewes, since at lambing time the farmer's flock was nearly doubled, but his grazing remained sufficient for only the original   55 number of sheep. The old mountain ewes are sold at the age of about five years to lowland farmers. By the time they have reached this age their teeth are worn down by years of hard grazing and their general condition is such that they can only be kept alive and lambing on richer pasture.   60

After the autumn sales, the flock is brought down from the mountain, the spring's lambs being wintered in the lowlands and the rest spending the winter in the fields around the farmhouse.

ISABEL EMMETT, *A North Wales Village. A Social Anthropological Study*
(Routledge and Kegan Paul)

1 Write a paragraph (of about 80 words) giving in order the main events of a mountain farmer's year.

2 Explain what is meant by 'the sheep's knowledge of the mountain' and explain why it is of such value to the farmer. Use about 80 words.

3 A dictionary explains the meanings of 'open' as:
  a not closed or blocked up
  b unfenced, unenclosed
  c exposed, bare
  d public
  e undisguised, manifest
Which of these meanings does the word have in l. 15? Briefly justify your choice.

Part Three
[*Time allowed: 1 hour*]

Read the following passage and then answer the questions. It concerns Richard I (nicknamed 'The Lionheart' or 'Cœur de Lion'), King of England from 1189 to 1199.

Richard, with all his characteristic virtues and faults cast in a
heroic mould, is one of the most fascinating medieval figures. He
has been described as the creature and embodiment of the age of
chivalry. In those days the lion was much admired in heraldry,
and more than one king sought to link himself with its repute.   5
When Richard's contemporaries called him 'Cœur de Lion' they
paid a lasting compliment to the king of beasts. Little did the
English people owe him for his services, and heavily did they pay
for his adventures. He was in England only twice for a few short
months in his ten years' reign; yet his memory has always stirred   10
English hearts, and seems to present throughout the centuries the
pattern of the fighting man. In all deeds of prowess as well as in
large schemes of war Richard shone. He was tall and delicately
shaped; strong in nerve and sinew, and most dextrous in arms.
He rejoiced in personal combat, and regarded his opponents   15
without malice as necessary agents in his fame. He loved war,
not so much for the sake of glory or political ends, but as other
men love science or poetry, for the excitement of the struggle and
the glow of victory. By this his whole temperament was toned;
and, united with the highest qualities of the military commander,   20
love of war called forth all the powers of his mind and body.

Although a man of blood and violence, Richard was too
impetuous to be either treacherous or habitually cruel. He was as
ready to forgive as he was hasty to offend; he was open-handed
and munificent to profusion; in war circumspect in design and   25
skilful in execution; in politics a child, lacking in subtlety and
experience. His political alliances were formed upon his likes and
dislikes; his political schemes had neither unity nor clearness of
purpose. The advantages gained for him by military genius were
flung away through diplomatic ineptitude. When, on the journey   30
to the East, Messina in Sicily was won by his arms he was easily
persuaded to share with his polished, faithless ally, Philip
Augustus, fruits of a victory which more wisely used might have
foiled the French King's artful schemes. The rich and tenable
acquisition of Cyprus was cast away even more easily than it   35
was won. His life was one magnificent parade, which, when ended,
left only an empty plain.

In 1199, when the difficulties of raising revenue for the endless
war were at their height, good news was brought to King Richard.
It was said there had been dug up near the castle of Chaluz, on the   40
lands of one of his French vassals, a treasure of wonderful
quality; a group of golden images of an emperor, his wife, sons

and daughters, seated round a table, also of gold, had been unearthed. The King claimed this treasure as lord paramount. The lord of Chaluz resisted the demand, and the King laid siege 45 to his small, weak castle. On the third day, as he rode daringly near the wall, confident in his hard-tried luck, a bolt from a crossbow struck him in the left shoulder by the neck. The wound, already deep, was aggravated by the necessary cutting out of the arrow-head. Gangrene set in, and Cœur de Lion 50 knew that he must pay a soldier's debt. He prepared for death with fortitude and calm, and in accordance with the principles he had followed. He arranged his affairs; he divided his personal belongings among his friends or bequeathed them to charity. He sent for his mother, the redoubtable Eleanor, who was at hand. 55 He declared John to be his heir, and made all present swear fealty to him. He ordered the archer who had shot the fatal bolt, and who was now a prisoner, to be brought before him. He pardoned him, and made him a gift of money. For seven years he had not confessed for fear of being compelled to be reconciled to 60 Philip, but now he received the offices of the Church with sincere and exemplary piety, and died in the forty-second year of his age on April 6, 1199, worthy, by the consent of all men, to sit with King Arthur and Roland and other heroes of martial romance at some Eternal Round Table, which we trust the Creator of the Universe 65 in His comprehension will not have forgotten to provide.

The archer was flayed alive.

SIR WINSTON CHURCHILL, *A History of the English-speaking Peoples,*
Volume I (Cassell)

After reading each of the following questions, choose the ONE correct answer, and indicate it by writing down the letter that stands for it. In all questions only ONE answer is correct. This is stressed in some questions, but remember that the rule applies to all of them.

1 'Characteristic' (l. 1) means

  A orthodox
  B distinctive
  C distinguished
  D well-known
  E dependable

2 In its context in l. 4 'chivalry' means

  A tournaments or hand-to-hand battle between knights
  B a devotion to the service of women

C an inclination to defend the weaker party
D leading cavalry charges in battle
E negotiations between kings

3 'Prowess' (l. 12) means

A display
B politics
C pride
D courage
E battle

4 That Richard spent so little time in England is a fact that the author

A virtually ignores
B makes light of
C emphasizes strongly
D tries to defend
E regrets bitterly

5 Richard lacked

A an angry temper
B an active ill-will
C a desire to tease
D aggressiveness
E circumspection

6 He was a poor

A king
B politician
C leader
D negotiator
E ally

7 'Tenable' (l. 34) means that Cyprus could have been

A sold quickly
B made useful
C retained easily
D valued highly
E developed economically

8 The author may exaggerate how easy it would have been for Richard to

A keep the lands he captured on his way to Palestine
B throw away the fruits of victory in Cyprus
C keep his promises to Philip Augustus
D capture Sicily
E claim the treasure found at Chaluz

9 The author regards Richard's near approach to the castle of Chaluz as

   A necessary and forced on him by circumstances
   B foolhardy and cocksure
   C brave and courageous
   D conceited and vain
   E tentative and exploratory

10 'Redoubtable' (l. 55) means

   A formidable
   B mercenary
   C estranged
   D trustworthy
   E neighbouring

11 Richard's behaviour as death approached showed

   A bravery and self-control
   B wisdom and correctness
   C devotion and over-generosity
   D chivalry and charity
   E fear of his spiritual future

12 'Little did the English people owe him for his services' (l. 7) means that the English

   A paid few taxes to him
   B gave him little respect
   C left undone few of their duties to him
   D had no real cause to feel grateful to him
   E received little protection from him against enemies near home

13 The 'pattern' (l. 12) means the

   A conventional example
   B example to·be slavishly copied
   C ideal example
   D example that summarizes the essentials
   E typical example

14 'Dextrous in arms' (l. 14) means

   A ingenious in his methods of fighting
   B subtle in his military tactics
   C skilful in using weapons
   D adaptable to different ways of fighting
   E an inventor of new weapons

15 Richard was kept from being habitually cruel by his

   A rashness

B moodiness
C caution
D meddlesomeness
E vindictiveness

16 To say that his life was a 'magnificent parade' (l. 36) implies that it was to some extent

    A spent chiefly at war
    B lived too pompously
    C impressive and admirable
    D an empty show
    E mere play-acting

17 The point of the last short paragraph is that Richard was

    A unable to influence the behaviour of his successors
    B more generous to his enemies than his associates were
    C cruelly resolved to be revenged on his enemies
    D cheated by his own family
    E a source of trouble even after his death

18 Which ONE of the following phrases is *not* used with a grim tinge of humour or irony?

    A 'good news was brought to King Richard' (l. 39)
    B 'his political alliances were formed upon his likes and dislikes' (ll. 27–8)
    C 'the redoubtable Eleanor' (l. 55)
    D 'which we trust the Creator of the Universe in His comprehension will not have forgotten to provide' (ll. 65–6)
    E 'the archer was flayed alive' (l. 67)

19 Which of the following phrases best describes Richard as seen by the author?

    A a brave king with minor faults
    B an aggressive king, too fond of war
    C a competent but quarrelsome soldier
    D a great general whose victories were important
    E a famous man who achieved a lot for England

20 The relationship between the first and second paragraph is that

    A each presents one side of the picture
    B both present Richard I's virtues mingled with his faults
    C the first says more about Richard's faults than the second
    D the first generalizes, the second gives examples
    E the second is the logical result of the first

21 Which ONE of the following words is used literally, *not* metaphorically?

   A 'mould' (l. 2)
   B 'stirred' (l. 10)
   C 'agents' (l. 16)
   D 'glow' (l. 19)
   E 'fruits' (l. 33)

Additional Question
[*Time allowed: 30 minutes*]

22 a What were Richard I's faults according to the author?
   b What were Richard I's virtues according to the author?
   c Explain why you feel (or do not feel) that the author stresses Richard's virtues more than his faults?
   d In what ways does the story of Richard's death prove some of the points that the author has already made?
   e By choosing two suitable examples, and commenting briefly on them, show how the author builds up a contrast between two successive phrases or sentences.

Paper 6

Part One

[*Time allowed: 1 hour*]

Write a composition on *one* of the following subjects:

a A school cruise.
b Write a description of a football match or any sports fixture which was interrupted by the violence of spectators.
c 'A man is known by the company he keeps.' (You may treat this as a title inviting a narrative or discussion.)
d 'It is better to be educated in a small school than in a large school.'
e Write to your local newspaper criticizing the failure to hold a local carnival this year. Point out the consequences.
f Describe a weekly or monthly magazine that you consider suitable for teenagers. Give your reasons for recommending it.
g Write a speech proposing that *either* pupils should have more say in running schools *or* better camping facilities should be provided for gypsies.
h Disaster.

Part Two

[*Time allowed: 1 hour*]

Read the following passages and then answer the questions.

Passage A concerns Louis XIV of France (reigned 1643–1715) and
Passage B concerns Edward VII of Britain (reigned 1901–10).

[A] As the embodiment of majesty and earthly power, Louis was popular. The French were delighted with him, and other European peoples were impressed. He was *the* king: just what a king ought to be. It has been said that Louis XIV was the 'greatest actor of majesty that ever filled a throne'. We are still prone to think of a   5
king as what is suggested by the name and demeanour of Louis XIV. Other monarchs did their best to emulate him, especially in outward appearances, deportment, and manners. Collectively, these manifestations may be expressed in the term 'etiquette'. Much of the etiquette practised at the court of Louis XIV was   10

doubtless inherited from Hapsburg tradition. Some of its forms lingered on, at Vienna, among the Austrian branch of the Hapsburgs, until the death of the Emperor Francis Joseph in 1916.

To us it seems absurd that a monarch, who is, after all, only a man, should rise from his bed every morning with a formal   15
ceremony (*levée*) in which crowds of the highest dignitaries in the land performed the duties of valets. Princes and dukes handed him his underwear, shoes, shirts, and other garments; lesser lords and ladies pushed and shoved with eagerness to attain the great honour of simply being present! It seems ridiculous   20
that this same formality and publicity should attend him at his meals, at most of his play, during his hours of work, and finally, when he retired for the night. But it must be remembered that such formalities are inseparable from an office as exalted as that of a divine-right monarch. To impress his subjects, to create   25
atmosphere, and to give a sense of reality to the claims which monarchy advanced, all these were necessary. That such pro-cedure was impressive is undoubtedly true. It is still so. The glamour which attends a crown, the fascination which surrounds royalty, may be seen today in the interest of the masses of the   30
British people in their royal dynasty—not to mention the interest of the American people in the personal affairs of both European royalty and of their own citizens of 'high degree'.

Despite the influence of democratic ideas and the limitations which have been placed by constitutions upon the powers of   35
kings, the persons and etiquette of royalty are still factors with which to conjure. The king's person is still a mighty symbol; his life and daily activities still command devoted attention. He is still surrounded by much mystery; he is still a majesty, aloof from other men; he is still surrounded by titles and some functions   40
which are reminiscent of the days of Louis XIV. As for the passionate avidity with which people sought the honour of attendance at levees, we may easily comprehend this by observing the twentieth-century press and its catering to the popular demands for intimate and personal details of the lives of those   45
who attain any form of publicity by means much more ridiculous, frequently, than having been born a king.

LAURENCE BRADFORD PACKARD, *The Age of Louis XIV*
(Holt, Rinehart and Winston, Inc.)

[**B**] Edward VII loved an excuse to dress up in uniform, inherited perhaps from the Hanoverian Family, for it was a well-known characteristic of King George IV. He loved pageantry, and woe betide the courtier or lord who deviated by the position of even the obscurest star from what was correct. He gave the somewhat 5 nonchalant Duke of Devonshire a piece of his mind for daring to appear wearing an order upside down, and the immaculate Rosebery was once reproved for appearing at a function looking like an American diplomat. A very true appraisement of this side of the king is again to be found in the diary of Wilfrid Blunt. 10 The two men were contemporaries, though as Blunt says, 'I had never much to do with him directly.' But Blunt—the enemy of imperialism and of everything conventional in his native land (except perhaps the enjoyment of country-house life)—is a commentator whom we should heed. He writes on the day, 20th 15 May 1910, when the king was buried:

> He had a passion for pageantry and ceremonial and dressing-up, and he was never tired of putting on uniforms and taking them off, and receiving princes and ambassadors and opening museums and hospitals, and attending cattle shows and military 20 shows and shows of every kind, while every night of his life he was to be seen at theatres and operas and music-halls.

The last is a slight exaggeration, though the novelist Robert Hichens, the author of *The Garden of Allah*, could write of the king in his reminiscences: 25

> The Edwardian age through which I lived was certainly very attractive to me. Night after night as I sat in my stall at the opera and saw him coming into the omnibus box and taking up his opera glasses to survey the glittering women in the first and ground tier boxes I saw a man who looked, I thought, extremely 30 genial and satisfied with his position in the scheme of the world.

He was like some splendidly plumed bird who seems to ask nothing more from existence than to be seen and admired, as he moved from London to Scotland, from Windsor to Portsmouth, from Sandringham to Yorkshire, from Goodwood to Doncaster. 35 His mother moved almost furtively through the British Isles: about King Edward there was nothing furtive, all was open and publicity was welcomed. He liked all men to know where he was and what he was up to. That was one reason why journalists loved him. He was never the least 'stand-offish', and he thoroughly 40 enjoyed being snapshot.

SIMON NOWELL-SMITH (editor), 'Edwardian England' from
The King by Roger Fulford (O.U.P.)

1 Compare life at the courts of Louis XIV and Edward VII, bringing out both the similarities and the differences.
2 What impressions have you formed of the characters and personalities of the two monarchs?
3 To what extent do both biographers admire and approve of the kings they write about?

In all questions credit will be given for arrangement of ideas, clear expression and direct comparison.

Part Three

[*Time allowed: 1 hour*]

Read the following passage (which for your convenience has been divided into two sections) and then answer the questions.

[A] Most West African lorries are not in what one would call the first flush of youth, and I had learnt by bitter experience not to expect anything very much of them. But the lorry that arrived to take me up to the mountains was worse than anything I had seen before: it tottered on the borders of senile decay. It stood 5 there on buckled wheels, wheezing and gasping with exhaustion from having to climb up the gentle slope to the camp, and I consigned myself and my loads to it with some trepidation. The driver, who was a cheerful fellow, pointed out that he would require my assistance in two very necessary operations: first, 10 I had to keep the hand brake pressed down when travelling downhill, for unless it was held thus almost level with the floor it sullenly refused to function. Secondly, I had to keep a stern eye on the clutch, a wilful piece of mechanism, that seized every chance to leap out of its socket with a noise like a strangling 15 leopard. As it was obvious that not even a West African lorry-driver could be successful in driving while crouched under the dashboard, I had to take over control of those instruments if I valued my life. So, while I ducked at intervals to put on the brake, amid the rich smell of burning rubber, our noble lorry 20 jerked its way towards the mountains at a steady twenty miles per hour; sometimes, when a downward slope favoured it, it threw caution to the winds and careered along in a madcap fashion at twenty-five.

[B] For the first thirty miles the red earth road wound its way through the lowland forest, the giant trees standing in solid

ranks alongside and their branches entwined in an archway of
leaves above us. Flocks of hornbills flapped across the road,
honking like the ghosts of ancient taxis, and on the banks,   5
draped decoratively in the patches of sunlight, the agama lizards
lay, blushing into sunset colouring with excitement and nodding
their heads furiously. Slowly and almost imperceptibly the road
started to climb upwards, looping its way in languid curves
round the forested hills. In the back of the lorry the boys lifted   10
up their voices in song:

> Home again, home again,
> When shall I see ma home?

The driver hummed the refrain softly to himself glancing at me to
see if I would object. To his surprise I joined in and so while the   15
lorry rolled onwards trailing a swirling tail of red dust behind it,
the boys in the back maintained the chorus while the driver and I
harmonized and sang complicated twiddly bits, and the driver
played a staccato accompaniment on the horn.

Breaks in the forest became more frequent the higher we   20
climbed, and presently a new type of undergrowth began to
appear: massive tree-ferns standing in conspiratorial groups at
the roadside on their thick, squat, hairy trunks, the fronds of
leaves sprouting from the tops like delicate, green fountains.
These ferns were the guardians of a new world, for suddenly, as   25
though the hills had shrugged themselves free of a cloak, the
forest disappeared. It lay behind us in the valley, a thick pelt of
green undulating away into the heat-shimmered distance, while
above us the hillside rose majestically, covered in a coat of
rippling, waist-high grass, bleached golden by the sun. The lorry   30
crept higher and higher, the engine gasping and shuddering
with this unaccustomed activity. I began to think that we should
have to push the wretched thing up the last two or three hundred
feet, but to everyone's surprise we made it, and the lorry crept on
to the brow of the hill, trembling with fatigue, spouting steam   35
from its radiator like a dying whale. We crawled to a standstill
and the driver switched off the engine.

'We must wait small-time, engine get hot,' he explained,
pointing to the forequarters of the lorry, which were by now
completely invisible under a cloud of steam. Thankfully I   40
descended from the red-hot inside of the cab and strolled down
to where the road dipped into the next valley. From this vantage
point I could see the country we had travelled through and the
country we were about to enter.

Behind lay the vast green forest, looking from this distance as   45
tight and impenetrable as lambs' wool; only on the hill-tops was
there any apparent break in the smooth surface of those millions
of leaves, for against the sky the trees were silhouetted in a tattered
fringe. Ahead of us lay a world so different that it seemed incredible that the two should be found side by side. There was no   50
gradual merging: behind lay the forest of huge trees, each clad in
its robe of polished leaves, glittering like green and gigantic
pearly kings: ahead, to the furthermost dim blue horizon, lay
range after range of hills, merging and folding into one another
like great frozen waves, tilting their faces to the sun, covered   55
from valley to crest with a rippling fur of golden-green grass that
paled or darkened as the wind curved and smoothed it. Behind
us, the forest was decked out in the most vivid of greens and
scarlets—harsh and intense colours. Before us, in this strange
mountain world of grass, the colours were soft and delicate—   60
fawns, pale green, warm browns and golds.

GERALD DURRELL, *The Bafut Beagles* (Hart-Davis)

After reading each of the following questions, choose the ONE correct
answer, and indicate it by writing down the letter that stands for it. In all
questions only ONE answer is correct. This is stressed in some questions,
but remember that the rule applies to all of them.

From Section A

1 'Senile decay' (l. 5) means

  A complete collapse
  B fatal wear and tear
  C enfeeblement through old age
  D utter uselessness
  E growing obsolescence

2 'Trepidation' (l. 8) means

  A intense terror
  B moderate alarm
  C undignified nervousness
  D diffident hesitation
  E growing surprise

3 Which ONE of the following words is used literally, *not* metaphorically?

  A 'flush' (l. 2)
  B 'borders' (l. 5)
  C 'gasping' (l. 6)
  D 'operations' (l. 10)
  E 'leap' (l. 15)

4 'Wilful' (l. 14) means

  A unruly
  B disobedient
  C eccentric
  D uncontrollable
  E headstrong

5 Which ONE of the following words does *not* help to suggest that the lorry (or part of it) is a living human?

  A 'flush' (l. 2)
  B 'tottered' (l. 5)
  C 'sullenly' (l. 13)
  D 'function' (l. 13)
  E 'madcap' (l. 23)

6 The author regarded the inadequacies of the lorry as

  A unimportant and trivial
  B welcome and interesting
  C novel and unexpected
  D dangerous and frightening
  E inevitable and amusing

7 The following words are used with a tinge of humour with the ONE EXCEPTION of

  A 'wheezing' (l. 6)
  B 'stern' (l. 13)
  C 'strangling' (l. 15)
  D 'instruments' (l. 18)
  E 'madcap' (l. 23)

From Section B

8 'Imperceptibly' (l. 8) means

  A with unexpected suddenness
  B in a series of steps
  C by unnoticed degrees
  D in gentle curves
  E with a weary hesitation

9 Which ONE of the following statements about metaphors is *not* true?

  A 'ranks' (l. 3) compares the trees beside the road to lines of soldiers drawn up on parade
  B 'blushing' (l. 7) compares the lizards to the cheeks of humans
  C 'tail' (l. 16) compares the dust to the tail of a bird
  D 'disappeared' (l. 27) compares the forest to a stage magician who disappears
  E 'pelt' (l. 27) compares the leaves of the forest to an animal's fur

10 Which ONE of the following comments on punctuation is *not* true?

  A there ought to be the same comma before 'glancing' (l. 14) as before 'looping' (l. 9) because both sentences are similar in structure

  B the comma after 'taxis' (l. 5) marks a more definite division in the sense than does any other comma in this sentence (ll. 4–8)

  C the colon in l. 22 introduces a list

  D 'trembling with fatigue' (l. 35) is an aside or parenthesis

  E 'which . . . . steam' (ll. 39–40) is preceded by a comma because it is a descriptive clause, not a defining one

11 Each of the following words carries on the suggestion that the lorry is human (or perhaps a horse) with the ONE EXCEPTION of

  A 'crept' (l. 31)

  B 'gasping' (l. 31)

  C 'shuddering' (l. 31)

  D 'trembling' (l. 35)

  E 'spouting' (l. 35)

12 In which of the following ways were the lowland and highland zones contrasted?

  i one had forests, the other grass

  ii one had brilliant colours, the other pale ones

  iii one was completely flat, the other full of steep hills

  iv one looked green and scarlet; the other had had its colour taken out by the sun

  v one seemed still, the other was more wind-swept

Which ONE of the following gives the correct statements?

  A i, ii and iv

  B i, ii, iii and iv

  C i, ii, iii and v

  D i, ii, iv and v

  E all of them

13 'Incredible' (l. 49) means

  A surprising

  B amazing

  C unbelievable

  D startling

  E irreconcilable

14 'Silhouetted' (l. 48) means

  A emphasized

B outlined
C waving
D obscured
E shadowed

15 'Decked out in' (l. 58) means
A sprinkled liberally with
B coloured gaily with
C made dramatic by
D dressed decoratively in
E covered completely by

16 The following pairs of words emphasize contrasts with the ONE EXCEPTION of
A 'behind' (l. 45) . . . . . . 'ahead' (l. 49)
B 'harsh' (l. 59) . . . . . . 'intense' (l. 59)
C 'vivid' (l. 58) . . . . . . 'delicate' (l. 60)
D 'forest' (l. 51) . . . . . . 'hills' (l. 54)
E 'robe' (l. 52) . . . . . . 'fur' (l. 56)

From the Whole Passage
17 A suitable title for the whole passage would be
A The wild West African lorry
B A comic ride in West Africa
C From the forests to the hills by lorry
D The exhausted lorry
E A journey that scared me

18 Which ONE of the following remarks could *not* be fairly made about the author's treatment of the lorry?
A it is the main topic of the first paragraph (ll. A.1–24)
B it is completely ignored in the second paragraph (ll. B.1–19)
C it is forgotten until near the end of the third paragraph (ll. B.20–37)
D it is a minor topic in the fourth paragraph (ll. B.38–44)
E it is completely forgotten in the fifth paragraph (ll. B.45–61)

19 We can deduce that the author was
A a little surprised to have to help drive the lorry
B not very interested in animal, bird and insect life
C unfriendly towards the natives
D bored by the appearance of the grasslands ahead
E reluctant to do any walking in so hot a climate

20 Which ONE of the following quotations is *not* likely to be from the same book?

    A 'From then onwards the road resembled a switchback, and we rattled and squeaked our way down into the valleys.'

    B 'I noticed in the valley ahead a village, looking at that distance like an irregular patch of black toadstools against the green.'

    C 'The hills and woods cast shadows; the pools of mist in the valleys gathered the moonbeams in cold, shivery light.'

    D 'The river moves along majestically, its brown waters full of hippo and crocodile, and the warm air above it filled with hawking swallows, blue and orange and white.'

    E 'The Cross River picks its way down from the mountains, until it runs sprawling and glittering into the great bowl of forest land around Mamfe.'

Additional Question
[*Time allowed: 45 minutes*]

21 Answer the following questions in your own words as far as possible.

From Section A

a Refer to instances where the author creates humour by describing the lorry, or part of it, as though it were a living person.

From Section B

b What additional meaning does the author achieve by using the following verbs instead of more usual ones:
'flapped' (l. 4); 'draped' (l. 6); 'blushing' (l. 7); 'looping' (l. 9).

c Give in a word or a short phrase the meaning of:
'entwined' (l. 3); 'languid' (l. 9); 'conspiratorial' (l. 22); 'undulating' (l. 28).

d Describe the contrast between the two types of African scenery.

e Bring out the force of this statement that 'there was no gradual merging' (l. 50).

From the Whole Passage

f Choose three similes. Discuss whether they make the author's descriptions more interesting or clearer or both.

g Quote four metaphors and in each case explain what two things are being compared.

h How can you tell that the author enjoyed the ride?

Paper 7

Part One
[*Time allowed: 1 hour*]

Write a composition on *one* of the following subjects:
a A blessing in disguise.
b 'Day after day, day after day,
We stuck, nor breath nor motion;
As idle as a painted ship
Upon a painted ocean.'
Write a description of a voyage, real or imaginary, during which you
were becalmed. Bring out the monotony and tedium of the experience.
c The problems of racial prejudice and how to solve them.
d Write a report suitable for a school magazine detailing the changes
that have taken place in your school during the past two years.
e The advantages and disadvantages of decimalization and metrication.
Distinguish long-term from short-term effects.
f November 5th. (This can be the title of a story or a discussion about the
celebration of this date with fireworks.)
g Antiques.
h Write a story, a description or an essay suggested by any *one* of the
illustrations on the two previous pages or on the title-page at the
beginning of the book. (Your composition may be directly about the
subject of the illustration, or may take only some suggestions from it,
but there must be some clear connection between the illustration and the
composition.)

Part Two
[*Time allowed: 1 hour*]

Read the following review of a book about a famous spy and then answer
the questions.

Books about spying tend to be even more untruthful than books
about sex. Thus—to take an extreme case—the odious Bond and
his ridiculous adventures are about as unlike the genuine article
as it is possible to imagine. How pleasant, then, to find in *The
Case of Richard Sorge* a superbly painstaking, factual and just   5
account of one of the most interesting affairs of the kind ever to

become known. Messrs. Deakin and Storry have examined all the sources, interviewed all the survivors, gathered together and sorted out every scrap of relevant information, and presented the whole with the dispassionate orderliness of the best kind of dossier.   10

Sorge, of mixed German and Russian parentage, and brought up in an affluent middle-class Berlin home, was just old enough to fight in the 1914-18 War. As a child and youth he accepted unquestioningly the mystique of German nationalism, but as a result of his wartime experiences, and of the chaos which followed, he moved steadily leftwards, and in due course became a Communist Party member.   15

His considerable intellectual gifts made him at first a teacher rather than an activist, but in time he became a full-fledged *apparatchik* working for the Red Army Fourth Bureau as a spy. Also, as an Intelligence agent he did not need to concern himself with Stalin's purges, soon in full swing. One after another of his bosses were shot over him, but their demises do not appear to have unduly distressed or disturbed him.   20   25

In any case he had the right temperament. It might be pleasant to believe that spies are all either fanatics for the cause they serve or suborned men: in actual fact, they mostly enjoy and choose the life. Even more than newspaper correspondents, they are their own masters. No one can check either the information they transmit or their expenses. When they have occasion to bribe a government official or a policeman they cannot be expected to produce a receipt; if they report that the Under-Secretary for Marine told them that fertilizer production was down on last year, it must be taken on trust. The deceptions they have to practise, the lies they have to tell, are congenial to naturally deceitful and romantic temperaments. If they are womanizers— as Sorge was—they can engage in endless seductions in the way of business, and charge them up to expenses. Even the booze which lubricates their passions and loosens their tongues is a professional requirement rather than a private indulgence.   30   35   40

Sorge's first espionage assignment was in China, where he had journalistic cover. This served him well, then and subsequently. He was obviously a capital journalist in the serious German style.   45

After China he went to Japan, and it was there that he really distinguished himself. Through his close liaison with the German Embassy he got access to very high grade Intelligence indeed,

which enabled him to keep Moscow apprised of Japan's
intentions, providing the Soviet High Command with an in- 50
valuable assurance that a Japanese attack was not to be expected
in Siberia since the decision had already been taken to fight a
Pacific war against America and Britain.

On October 18th, 1941 Sorge was arrested by the Japanese as a
result of a chance disclosure by one of his minor agents. There 55
followed a long period of interrogation in which Sorge admitted
that he was 'an agent of international Communism', and dis-
closed something—as little as possible—of his Tokyo set-up.
Sorge was convinced right up to the end that, in view of his great
achievements as a spy, and of his importance vis-à-vis the 60
Japanese, the Soviet Government would intercede on his behalf
and an exchange be arranged.

The Soviet Embassy in Tokyo, however, held scrupulously
aloof from the whole affair, and Sorge was duly executed on (a
typical Japanese touch) the twenty-seventh anniversary of the 65
Russian Revolution—November 7th, 1944. Had he been sent
back to the U.S.S.R. there can be little doubt that he would
likewise have been liquidated there. Stalin intensely disliked
foreigners, especially those who had served the Communist
cause abroad. Twenty years later a different wind was blowing in 70
Moscow; Sorge was posthumously awarded the highest Soviet
decoration—Hero of the Soviet Union—and a street was named
after him; also a submarine.

The character of Sorge is by no means unattractive or un-
impressive. His Japanese interrogator said of him, 'I have never 75
met anyone as great as he was', and his Japanese mistress,
Hanako-san, spoke affectionately and admiringly of him. With
uncommon skill he managed to meet the requirements of three
masters—the Fourth Bureau, the German Embassy and the
German newspaper *Frankfurter Zeitung,* using different versions 80
of the same material for each of them.

Hanako-san reports that on the day he heard of the German
attack on Russia he burst into floods of weeping, bitterly re-
calling that he had passed to the Fourth Bureau the most specific
report on its imminence. This, like other similar warnings 85
Stalin received, was filed away under the heading 'Doubtful and
misleading information'.

It is interesting that great Intelligence coups are rarely service-
able. We were excellently informed on German rearmament.
Stalin was given the date and time of the German attack, Hitler 90

had the plans and order of battle for the Allied invasion of Europe: but the hands which received this information still remained nerveless. It looks as though Intelligence has to be trivial and phoney to be usable. Poor Sorge!

MALCOLM MUGGERIDGE, *The Observer Foreign News Service*

After reading each of the following questions, choose the ONE correct answer, and indicate it by writing down the letter that stands for it. In all questions only ONE answer is correct. This is stressed in some questions, but remember that the rule applies to all of them.

1 The purpose of the first paragraph (ll. 1–11) is to
   A point out the improbable events in novels about spies
   B persuade the reader to dislike spies, including Sorge
   C contrast truthful and unrealistic books about spies
   D suggest that even the best books about spies are often inaccurate
   E express a distaste for spying

2 'Odious' (l. 2) means
   A unrealistic
   B fictitious
   C hateful
   D reprehensible
   E far-fetched

3 Which of the following qualities does the reviewer attribute to Sorge?
      i intelligence
     ii callousness
    iii cheerfulness
     iv skill as a journalist
      v remorse

   Which ONE of the following gives the correct qualities?
   A i, ii and iii
   B i, iii and iv
   C i, iv and v
   D i, ii, iii and iv
   E all of them

4 Which of the following quotations from a book about Sorge is nearest in spirit to the attitude which the reviewer adopts towards him in his review?
   A 'On his gravestone the inscription reads: "Here sleeps a brave warrior who devoted his life to opposing war."'

B 'The fate of three nations rested upon the information which Richard Sorge was sending out of the German Embassy.'

C 'The most notorious spy in Russian history.'

D 'On November 7th, 1944, the anniversary of the Russian Revolution, Richard Sorge walked to his execution, in lonely isolation.'

E 'He convinced the Russians in 1941 that the Japanese would attack the Americans but not the Russians.'

5 The reviewer argues that facts discovered by spies

A change history decisively

B rarely make any real difference

C are usually trivial and 'phoney'

D are doubtful and misleading

E make history more romantic

6 The reviewer pities Sorge because

A Stalin, whom he served, secretly disliked foreigners

B he was disappointed not to be exchanged by the Russians

C his Japanese mistress loved him so sincerely

D Stalin ignored most—perhaps all—of the news he discovered

E he was appalled at the German attack on Russia

7 'Dispassionate' (l. 10) means without

A emotional bias

B real enthusiasm

C warm indignation

D any glamour

E crude sensationalism

8 'Mystique' (l. 15) means

A air of mystery

B national prejudices

C group of traditions

D patriotic idealism

E imaginative fervour

9 'Demises' (l. 24) means

A disappearances

B removals

C crimes

D deaths

E dismissals

10 'Liquidated' (l. 68) means

   A executed
   B toasted
   C given drink
   D dismissed
   E menaced

11 'Nerveless' (l. 93) means

   A cool
   B unfrightened
   C overconfident
   D irresolute
   E weak

12 'Capital' (l. 44) means

   A capable
   B leading
   C very good
   D metropolitan
   E fluent

13 Which ONE of the following is *not* a colloquial word and is *not* used to convey disrespect?

   A 'article' (l. 3)
   B 'affluent' (l. 13)
   C 'bosses' (l. 24)
   D 'booze' (l. 39)
   E 'phoney' (l. 94)

14 'Suborned men' (l. 28) are men who are

   A fanatical
   B born liars
   C dedicated to a cause
   D bribed
   E intimidated

15 Which ONE of the following sentences or phrases is *not* intended to ridicule or condemn spying?

   A 'Books about spying tend to be even more untruthful than books about sex' (l. 1)
   B 'Also, as an Intelligence agent he did not need to concern himself with Stalin's purges' (l. 22)
   C 'When they . . . . . . bribe . . . . a policeman they cannot be expected to produce a receipt' (ll. 31–3)
   D 'If they report . . . . . . it must be taken on trust' (ll. 33–5)
   E 'His Japanese interrogator said of him, "I have never met anyone as great as he was"' (ll. 75–6)

16 'Affluent' (l. 13) means

    A comfortable
    B sophisticated
    C patriotic
    D rich
    E commercially-minded

17 Which ONE of the following statements is *not* true?

    A the dashes in l. 2 give emphasis to the words in between them
    B the comma in l. 24 is permissible but not essential
    C the colon in l. 28 helps contrast two statements
    D the semi-colon in l. 33 shows that there is a contrast between the two halves of the sentence
    E in ll. 29 and 46 the commas are not essential

18 All the following points are made by the reviewer to criticize the Russians or the Communists with the ONE EXCEPTION that

    A Stalin ignored Sorge's warning that Hitler would invade Russia
    B Russia did not try to save Sorge by an exchange of prisoners
    C Stalin would probably have liquidated Sorge
    D twenty years after his death the Russians honoured Sorge
    E Stalin shot a series of heads of the Russian spy organization

19 The reviewer regards Sorge as fundamentally

    A competent and skilful
    B important historically
    C selfish and pleasure-loving
    D a German patriot
    E attractive to women

20 Which ONE of the following words is *not* used to praise some attribute of Sorge?

    A 'interesting' (l. 6)
    B 'gifts' (l. 19)
    C 'womanizer' (l. 37)
    D 'capital' (l. 44)
    E 'uncommon' (l. 78)

Additional Question
[*Time allowed: 45 minutes*]

21 a In what way was this factual book about Sorge unlike most novels written about spies?
    b Comment on this reviewer's occasional use of undignified or colloquial language. What effects does he achieve by it?

c Comment on three details which the reviewer includes in order to satirize the Communist Party.

d What were the two principal pieces of information that Sorge gave Stalin, and what use did Stalin make of them?

e What justifications are there for ending this review with the comment, 'Poor Sorge!'?

f What virtues or accomplishments does this review attribute to Sorge?

g Discuss briefly whether the first and fourth paragraphs give rather contradictory pictures of spying as a trade.

h What does the reviewer tell us about the worse side of Sorge's character?

Paper 8

Part One

[*Time allowed: 1 hour*]

Write a composition on *one* of the following subjects:

a Write a story entitled 'Three's company'.
b 'The flannelled fools at the wickets, or the muddied oafs at the goals'.
   Do you think that games are for those who don't read and can't think?
c The raising of the school-leaving age.
d How would you solve the parking problem in large towns?
e 'Crabbed Age and Youth
   Cannot live together.'
   What are the special problems of old and young people living in the same community?
f Drugs.

Part Two

Read the following passage and then answer the questions.

(In *My Early Life* Sir Winston Churchill describes how the Pathans, wild tribesmen on what was then the North-West frontier of India, loved to fight their neighbours. Although he writes in the present tense, he is describing the state of the frontier in the 1890's, and his view is an unsympathetic one.)

Campaigning on the Indian frontier is an experience by itself. Neither the landscape nor the people find their counterparts in any other portion of the globe. Valley walls rise steeply five or six thousand feet on every side. The columns crawl through a maze of giant corridors down which fierce snow-fed torrents foam   5
under skies of brass. Amid these scenes of savage brilliancy there dwells a race whose qualities seem to harmonize with their environment. Except at harvest-time, when self-preservation enjoins a temporary truce, the Pathan tribes are always engaged in private or public war. Every man is a warrior, a politician and a   10
theologian. Every large house is a real feudal fortress made, it is true, only of sun-baked clay, but with battlements, turrets, loopholes, flanking towers, drawbridges, etc, complete. Every

village has its defence. Every family cultivates its vendetta; every clan, its feud. The numerous tribes and combinations of 15
tribes all have their accounts to settle with one another. Nothing is ever forgotten, and very few debts are left unpaid. For the purposes of social life, in addition to the convention about harvest-time, a most elaborate code of honour has been established and is on the whole faithfully observed. A man who knew 20
it and observed it faultlessly might pass unarmed from one end of the frontier to another. The slightest technical slip would, however, be fatal. The life of the Pathan is thus full of interest; and his valleys, nourished alike by endless sunshine and abundant water, are fertile enough to yield with little labour the modest 25
material requirements of a sparse population.

Into this happy world the nineteenth century brought two new facts: the breech-loading rifle and the British Government. The first was an enormous luxury and blessing; the second, an unmitigated nuisance. The convenience of the breech-loading, 30
and still more of the magazine rifle, was nowhere more appreciated than in the Indian highlands. A weapon which would kill with accuracy at fifteen hundred yards opened a whole new vista of delights to every family or clan which could acquire it. One could actually remain in one's own house and fire at one's 35
neighbour nearly a mile away. One could lie in wait on some high crag, and at hitherto unheard-of ranges hit a horseman far below. Even villages could fire at each other without the trouble of going far from home. Fabulous prices were therefore offered for these glorious products of science. Rifle-thieves scoured all 40
India to reinforce the efforts of the honest smuggler. A steady flow of the coveted weapons spread its genial influence throughout the frontier, and the respect which the Pathan tribesmen entertained for Christian civilization was vastly enhanced.

The action of the British Government on the other hand was 45
entirely unsatisfactory. The great organizing, advancing, absorbing power to the southward seemed to be little better than a monstrous spoil-sport. If the Pathans made forays into the plains, not only were they driven back (which after all was no more than fair), but a whole series of subsequent interferences took place, 50
followed at intervals by expeditions which toiled laboriously through the valleys, scolding the tribesmen and exacting fines for any damage which they had done. No one would have minded these expeditions if they had simply come, had a fight and then gone away again. In many cases this was their practice under 55

what was called the 'butcher and bolt policy' to which the Government of India long adhered. But towards the end of the nineteenth century these intruders began to make roads through many of the valleys, and in particular the great road to Chitral. They sought to ensure the safety of these roads by threats, by forts and by subsidies. There was no objection to the last method   60 so far as it went. But the whole of this tendency to road-making was regarded by the Pathans with profound distaste. All along the road people were expected to keep quiet, not to shoot one another, and above all not to shoot at travellers along the road. It was too much to ask, and a whole series of quarrels took their   65 origin from this source.

SIR WINSTON CHURCHILL, *My Early Life* (The Hamlyn Publishing Group)

After reading each of the following questions, choose the ONE correct answer, and indicate it by writing down the letter that stands for it. In all questions only ONE answer is correct. This is stressed in some questions, but remember that the rule applies to all of them.

1 A 'vendetta' (l. 14) is a

   A cereal
   B religion
   C blood-feud
   D native custom
   E hereditary field

2 The debts referred to in l. 17 are

   A loans not repaid
   B barter not completed
   C good turns not returned
   D murders unavenged
   E grudges ignored

3 The Pathans welcomed the

   A spread of British rule
   B chance to make peace with another tribe
   C introduction of the breech-loading rifle
   D the extension of luxuries
   E spread of trade

4 In the sentence 'The first . . . . nuisance' (ll. 28–30) the author

   A gives his own views

   B criticizes the British Government

   C pretends to accept the Pathan point of view

   D condones rifle-thieves

   E contrasts the British and Pathan attitudes

5 In the first two paragraphs each of the following words is used in an ironical way (i.e. a bitter joke against the Pathans) with the ONE EXCEPTION of

   A 'campaigning' (l. 1)

   B 'interest' (l. 23)

   C 'happy' (l. 27)

   D 'delights' (l. 34)

   E 'glorious' (l. 40)

6 In the last paragraph the most ironical word is

   A 'action' (l. 45)

   B 'unsatisfactory' (l. 46)

   C 'spoil-sport' (l. 48)

   D 'toiled' (l. 51)

   E 'interferences' (l. 50)

7 Which ONE of the following is *not* one of the geographical facts about North-West India?

   A melting snows

   B steep hillsides

   C bright sunshine

   D a large population

   E fertile valleys

8 Use of certain words suggests that it would be very difficult to travel through Pathan territory without being killed; these words do *not* include

   A 'convention about harvest-time' (l. 18)

   B 'elaborate' (l. 19)

   C 'on the whole' (l. 20)

   D 'faultlessly' (l. 21)

   E 'slightest technical slip' (l. 22)

9 Which ONE of the following was *not* an activity that the improved types of rifle made easier for the Pathan villagers?

   A killing men at long range

   B shooting from one's own house

   C lying in ambush on a high rock

    D shooting horsemen in remote valleys
    E dispensing with the services of smugglers

10 'Forays' (l. 48) means

    A intrusions
    B explorations
    C advances
    D raids
    E marches

11 Building roads by the British

    A put an end to a whole series of quarrels
    B reduced the Pathans' opportunities to carry on feuds
    C lessened the subsidies paid to the Pathans
    D was part of the 'butcher and bolt' policy
    E gave the Pathans a quieter life

12 Which ONE of the following words is used literally, *not* metaphorically?

    A 'fabulous' (l. 39)
    B 'scoured' (l. 40)
    C 'reinforce' (l. 41)
    D 'efforts' (l. 41)
    E 'flow' (l. 41)

13 'Absorbing' (l. 46) means that the British Government in India

    A was obsessed with the need to think about improving India
    B was capable of remaining uninjured by Pathan raids
    C kept annexing other parts of India to those parts which it ruled directly
    D continually prevented the Pathans from leading their natural life
    E deliberately tried to put an end to native customs

14 Smugglers are called 'honest' (l. 41) because they

    A carried on the trade traditional in their tribe and family
    B were less reprehensible than people who actually stole arms
    C sincerely held political views opposed to the British
    D were quite candid to everyone, even to British officials, about how they earned their living
    E are the targets of the author's indignation

15 A suitable title for the extract would be

    A Campaigning on the North-West frontier
    B Murderous rifle-thieves and honest smugglers
    C Why the Pathans resented the British Government's policies
    D The popularity of improved rifles among the Pathans
    E Trigger-happy natives in a happy sunny world

16 The most serious fault of the first sentence (l. 1) is that it

   A fails to prepare the reader for the unique conditions of the North-West frontier

   B ignores how much India changed between the events described (1896) and the writing of the book (1930)

   C underrates the similarity of all guerrilla wars

   D is partly out of step with the next two paragraphs

   E merely reduplicates the idea of the second sentence

17 'The slightest technical slip' referred to in l. 22 would be a slip in

   A navigation

   B use of a weapon

   C pronunciation

   D etiquette

   E religious observance

18 All the following groups of words deliberately contain slang or colloquial elements in order to ridicule the Pathans with the ONE EXCEPTION of

   A 'flanking towers, drawbridges, etc' (l. 13)

   B 'an unmitigated nuisance' (l. 30)

   C 'fabulous prices' (l. 39)

   D 'a monstrous spoil-sport' (l. 47)

   E 'profound distaste' (l. 62)

19 Which ONE of the following statements about comparisons is *not* correct?

   A in l. 3 the sides of valleys are compared to the sides of buildings

   B in l. 5 narrow passes between mountains are compared to narrow passage-ways inside buildings

   C in l. 4 the columns advancing slowly through passes are compared to a reptile moving in a position that is not erect

   D in l. 5 the snow added to a stream is compared to food given to a person eating

   E in l. 34 the series of pleasures that a Pathan could enjoy with an improved rifle are compared to a series of delights, increasing in intensity

20 'Brilliancy' (l. 6) refers to the

   A Pathan civilization

   B bravery of the tribesman

   C colourful clothes worn by Pathans

   D dramatic climate and landscape of the North-West frontier

   E military genius of the Pathans

21 The 'butcher and bolt policy' of the British (l. 56) means that the British

   A invaded the Pathans' territory permanently

   B were defeated and driven back by the Pathans

C carried out brief, punitive raids
D killed very many Pathans
E even murdered fugitives

22 The 'butcher and bolt policy' seemed to the Pathans
    A a new invention
    B a particularly hateful measure
    C economically illogical
    D likely to give them chances to steal rifles
    E preferable to enforcing a permanent peace

Additional Question
[*Time allowed: 30 minutes*]

23 a One sort of irony consists of saying the opposite of what you mean.
Comment on two occasions when the author uses this sort of irony.
  b Another sort of irony consists of pretending to agree with arguments
that you put forward, but exaggerating or distorting them so that
they will seem slightly ridiculous to your reader. Show how the
author makes use of this irony on a large scale in this passage.
  c When you read the passage for the first time, when did you first
become aware of the irony, and what aspect or phrase of the passage
first alerted you to the irony?
  d In what ways did the geography of the North-West frontier encourage
the Pathans to prolong their feuds?
  e Explain the meaning of the following words:
      'counterparts' (l. 2); 'columns' (l. 4); 'harmonize with' (l. 7); 'con-
vention' (l. 18); 'sparse' (l. 26); 'unmitigated' (l. 30).
  f Explain why the Pathans fell out with the British Government.

Paper 9

Part One

[Time allowed: 1 hour]

Write a composition on *one* of the following subjects:

a How have your years at school prepared you for your life after leaving school?
b The last straw.
c The day we moved to a new house.
d Must we bury ourselves in our own rubbish? You might deal with pollution, disposal of waste, litter, and disfigurement of town and countryside.
e 'Pop' singers.
f Typhoon.
g Black sheep.
h Television and radio plays as a reflection of real life.

Part Two

[Time allowed: 1 hour]

Read the following passage (which for your convenience has been divided into two sections) and then answer the questions.

[A] The speed with which a newly made-up rhyme can travel the length and breadth of the country by the schoolchild grapevine seems to be little short of miraculous. Some idea of the efficiency of oral transmission can be obtained by following verses which are topical, or which are parodies of newly published songs, 5 and can consequently be dated, although for test purposes it is, unfortunately, best to study specimens which are of a scurrilous or indelicate nature for with these there is, in general, less likelihood of dissemination by means other than word-of-mouth.

A notorious instance of the transmission of scurrilous verses 10 occurred in 1936 at the time of the Abdication. The word-of-mouth rhymes which then gained currency were of a kind which could not possibly, at that time, have been printed, broadcast, or

even repeated in the music halls. One verse, in particular, made
up one can only wonder by whom,   15

> Hark the Herald Angels sing,
> Mrs. Simpson's pinched our king,

was on juvenile lips not only in London, but as far away as
Chichester in the south, and Liverpool and Oldham in the north.
News that there was a constitutional crisis did not become   20
public property until around 25 November of that year, and the
king abdicated on 10 December. Yet at a school Christmas party
in Swansea given before the end of term, Christmas 1936, when
the tune played happened to be 'Hark the Herald Angels Sing', a
mistress found herself having to restrain her small children from 25
singing this lyric, known to all of them, which cannot have been
composed much more than three weeks previously. Many an
advertising executive with a six-figure budget at his disposal
might envy such crowd penetration. Similarly, the ultra juvenile
verse,   30

> Temptation, temptation, temptation,
> Dick Barton went down to the station
> Blondie was there
> All naked and bare,
> Temptation, temptation, temptation,   35

wherever it may have originated, was reported to us in quick
succession as rife among children in Kirkcaldy in January 1952,
as known to children in Swansea in January 1952, and it reached
children in Alton in February 1952. These three places are up to
400 miles apart; yet an instance of even more distant transmission 40
can be cited. At the beginning of 1956 'The Ballad of Davy
Crockett' was launched on the radio. It was especially intended to
appeal to children, and quickly reached the top of the adult hit
parade. But the official words of the ballad, beginning,

> Born on a mountain top in Tennessee,   45
> Greenest state in the Land of the Free,

were very small beer compared with the word-of-mouth stanzas
which rapidly won approval in juvenile society. One composition,
beginning 'The Yellow Rose of Texas', was collected in Perth in
April 1956, in Alton, Battersea, Great Bookham, Reading, and   50
Scarborough in July 1956, in Kent in August 1956, and in
Swansea in September 1956. Another parody sung by schoolgirls

in Swansea in September 1956 appeared to have local associations:

> Born on a table top in Joe's Café,   55
> Dirtiest place in the U.S.A.,
> Polished off his father when he was only three,
> Polished off his mother with D.D.T.
>> Davy, Davy Crockett,
>> King of the Wild Frontier.   60

The teacher who sent this verse remarked that Joe's Café was a popular Swansea establishment near the beach. Subsequently, however, we had news of the verse being current in Brentwood, Hornchurch, Reading, Upminster, and Woolwich, all naming 'Joe's Café'. But unknown to any of our home observers, and   65 before the official Davy Crockett song had reached Britain, an Australian correspondent, writing 3 January 1956, had reported that the following ditty was 'sweeping the schools' in Sydney:

> Reared on a paddle-pop in Joe's Café,
> The dirtiest dump in the U.S.A.,   70
> Poisoned his mother with D.D.T.
> And shot his father with a 303.
>> Davy, Davy Crockett,
>> The man who is no good.

It seems that the schoolchild underground also employs trans-   75
world couriers.

[B] The previous section has shown how quickly a rhyme passes from one schoolchild to the next and illustrates a further difference between school lore and nursery lore. In nursery lore a verse or tradition, learnt in early childhood, is not usually passed on again until the little listener has grown up, and has children of his   5
own, or even grandchildren. The period between learning a nursery rhyme and transmitting it may be anything from twenty to seventy years. With the playground lore, however, a rhyme may be excitedly passed on within the very hour it is learnt; and, in general, it passes between children who are the same age, or   10
nearly so, since it is uncommon for the difference in age between playmates to be more than five years. If, therefore, a playground rhyme can be shown to have been current for a hundred years, or even just for fifty, it follows that it has been retransmitted over and over again; very possibly it has passed along a chain of two   15
or three hundred young hearers and tellers, and the wonder is

that it remains alive after so much handling, let alone that it
bears resemblance to the original wording.

In most schools there is a wholly new generation of children
every six years; and when a rhyme such as 'Little fatty doctor,   20
how's your wife?' can be shown to be more than 130 years old
it may be seen that it has passed through the keeping of not less
than twenty successive generations of schoolchildren, and been
exposed to the same stresses that nursery lore would meet only
after 500 years of oral conveyance. This, in itself, makes school-   25
child lore of peculiar value to the student of oral communication,
for the behaviour and defects of oral transmission can be seen in
operation during a relatively short period, much as if the phenomenon had been placed in a mechanical stresser to speed up the
wear and tear.   30

Thus we find that variations, even apparently creative ones,
occur more often by accident than by design. Usually they come
about through mishearing or misunderstanding, as in the well-
known hymnal misapprehension:

Can a woman's tender care   35
Cease towards the child she-bear?

A line in the song 'I'm a knock-kneed sparrow' quickly becomes
'I'm a cockney sparrow', 'Calico breeches', no longer familiar
to youth today becomes 'comical breeches'. 'Elecampane'
becomes 'elegant pain'. 'Green gravel, green gravel' becomes by   40
association 'Greengages, greengages'. And the unmeaning
'Alligoshee, alligoshee', in the marching game, is rationalized to
'Adam and Eve went out to tea'. At one school the pledges 'Die on
oath', 'Dianothe', and 'Diamond oath' were all found to be
current at the same time. The common tendency to speed up a   45
ritual or abridge a formula also produces surprising results. At a
Surrey school the pledge 'Cub's honour' became, by jest, 'Cub's-
on-a-car', which was presently abridged, so that the standard
pledge became 'Car'.

IONA and PETER OPIE, *The Lore and Language of Schoolchildren*
(Clarendon Press)

After reading each of the following questions, choose the ONE correct answer, and indicate it by writing down the letter that stands for it. In all questions only ONE answer is correct. This is stressed in some questions, but remember that the rule applies to all of them.

From Section A

1 'Oral transmission' (l. 4) means the

  A spreading of rumours
  B popularity of naughty verses
  C tendency of children to recite the same rhymes
  D passing on of information by word-of-mouth
  E memorization and repetition of rhymes

2 These authors chose to investigate the passing on of scurrilous verses because they were

  A popular with children all over Britain
  B topical and easy to remember
  C an amusing example for their readers
  D less likely to have been printed or recited publicly
  E able to be traced to a definite date

3 'Currency' (l. 12) means

  A notoriety
  B attention
  C circulation
  D topicality
  E news value

4 'Crowd penetration' (l. 29) means the ability to

  A reach and fascinate large numbers of people
  B appeal to the emotions of crowds
  C attract the attention of crowds
  D win wide popularity
  E make popular comments on topical items of news

5 The *main* intention of Section A is to prove that

  A children love to write their own words to the tunes of popular songs
  B parodies of newly published songs can be dated
  C children's word-of-mouth rhymes spread quickly
  D children are no respecters of persons
  E children's comic versions of popular songs spread overseas

6 Which ONE of the following words is used literally, *not* metaphorically?
  A 'specimens' (l. 7)
  B 'hit' (l. 43)
  C 'parody' (l. 52)

D 'sweeping' (l. 68)
E 'dump' (l. 70)

7 'Rife' (l. 37) means

   A very popular
   B commonly occurring
   C frequently recited
   D currently numerous
   E universally popular

8 The metaphor 'did not become public property' (l. 20) suggests that news of the constitutional crisis was not

   A referred to in newspapers
   B widely revealed
   C the subject of gossip
   D generally believed
   E much satirized

9 'Cited' (l. 41) means

   A quoted in support of an argument
   B mentioned in passing
   C stressed as interesting
   D chosen as an illustration
   E referred to as an example

10 In its essentials Section A contains

   A three examples of the same basic fact, with only minor details different in each instance
   B three humorous examples of a serious point
   C three examples of American influence on British children
   D three examples of parody interspersed with serious comment
   E an idea and three examples, the last being the most surprising

11 'Very small beer' (l. 47) means

   A mildly amusing
   B too respectable
   C rather colloquial
   D comparatively dull
   E ineffectively obvious

From Section B

12 'Rationalized to' (l. 42) means

   A subtly translated into
   B made intelligible in the form of
   C shortened into fewer words as
   D translated into the modern form of
   E sensibly converted to

13 Variations in playground rhymes occur as a result of
     i deliberate changes by many children
    ii mishearing during oral transmission
   iii censorship by adults
   iv failure to understand the original version
    v shortening the original version

Which ONE of the following gives the correct reasons?
A ii, iv and v
B i and ii
C i and iii
D i, iv and v
E ii and iv

14 The word 'chain' (l. 15) compares hearers and tellers of school lore to
A fire-fighters passing buckets of water to one another
B the successive links in a bicycle chain
C connected series of metal links
D a firm serving many shops
E convicts being chained together

15 'Stresses' (l. 24) means
A changes in methods of emphasis
B vulnerable experiences
C a gradual deterioration
D powerful forces that slowly produce change
E intense pressures producing immediate change

16 'Peculiar' (l. 26) means
A considerable
B out of the way
C eccentric
D unexpected
E special

17 'Abridged' (l. 48) means
A changed
B transposed
C slurred
D shortened
E lessened

18 Which ONE of the following is *not* one of the main ideas about school lore in Section B?
A it is passed on to other children at once

B it is passed on to children of the same age
C it is passed on very frequently in any space of time
D it is often changed by the deliberate creativity of children
E its wording is usually changed only by accident

19 The second and third sentences, 'In nursery lore .... seventy years' (ll. 3–8)

   A are a conclusion drawn from the ideas in Section A
   B stress the contrast between nursery lore and playground rhymes
   C are another example of the ideas expounded in Section B
   D give an exception to the rule stated elsewhere in Section B
   E have no logical connection with the rest and should have been omitted

20 The 'defects of oral transmission' (l. 27) can be summed up under all of the following headings with the ONE EXCEPTION of

   A Changes in wording due to mishearing or misunderstanding
   B Traditional words replaced by more meaningful ones
   C Children are excited when they pass on what they have heard
   D Several versions of a tradition may survive together
   E Phrases and words are often shortened when being passed on

Additional Questions
[*Time allowed: 40 minutes*]

21 Explain the meaning of:
   a 'an advertising executive with a six-figure budget' (l. A. 28)
   b 'the official words of the ballad were very small beer compared with the word-of-mouth stanzas' (l. A. 44)
   c 'the schoolchild underground also employs transworld couriers' (l. A. 75)

22 Put into your own words 'the behaviour and defects of oral transmission can be seen during a relatively short period' (l. B. 27).

23 Account for the following marks of punctuation:
   a the hyphen between 'six' and 'figure' (l. A. 28)
   b the semi-colon after 'apart' (l. A. 40)
   c the inverted commas round 'The Ballad of Davy Crockett' (l. A. 41)
   d the inverted commas round 'sweeping the schools' (l. A. 68)

24 Name two qualities of parody.

Paper 10

Part One

[*Time allowed: 1 hour*]

Write a composition on *one* of the following subjects:

a Motorways. Discuss problems of planning, construction, use and maintenance.

b 'I leaned upon a coppice gate
When Frost was spectre-gray,
And Winter's dregs made desolate
The weakening eye of day.'
Write a description of a scene brought to your mind by these lines of Thomas Hardy.

c What descriptions of schooldays have you read in autobiography and fiction, and how do these compare with your own experiences?

d Vandalism: its causes and cures.

e Organized begging.

f In view of the huge distances involved, some method of temporarily arresting life, such as deep freezing, must be found before the programme of space exploration can be greatly expanded. What do you think about this? What are the possibilities of such a development?

g Write a story, a description or an essay suggested by any *one* of the illustrations on the two following pages. (Your composition may be directly about the subject of the illustration, or may take only some suggestions from it, but there must be some clear connection between the illustration and the composition.)

Part Two

[*Time allowed: 1 hour*]

Read the following article (which for your convenience has been divided into three sections) and then answer the questions.

A

[I] 'In every known human society the male's needs for achievement can be recognized . . . In a great number of human societies men's sureness of their sex role is tied up with their right, or ability, to practise some activity that women are not allowed to

'Of course, if you'd rather see your daughter going about in rags . . .'

'Turn her round and head for the amusement arcade.'

practise. Their maleness in fact has to be underwritten by pre-   5
venting women from entering some field or performing some feat.'
[II] This is the conclusion of the anthropologist Margaret Mead
about the way in which the roles of men and women in society
should be distinguished.
[III] If talk and print are considered it would seem that the   10
formal emancipation of women is far from complete. There is a
flow of publications about the continuing domestic bondage of
women and about the complicated system of defences which men
have thrown up around their hitherto accepted advantages,
taking sometimes the obvious form of exclusion from types of   15
occupation and sociable groupings, sometimes the more subtle
form of automatic doubt of the seriousness of women's pre-
tensions to the level of intellect and resolution that men, it is
supposed, bring to the business of running the world.
[IV] There are a good many objective pieces of evidence for the   20
erosion of men's status. In the first place, there is the widespread
postwar phenomenon of the woman Prime Minister, in India,
Ceylon and Israel.
[V] Secondly, there is the very large increase in the number of
women who work, especially married women and mothers of   25
children. More diffusely there are the increasingly numerous
convergences between male and female behaviour: the approximation to identical styles in dress and coiffure, the sharing
of domestic tasks, and the admission of women to all sorts of
hitherto exclusively male leisure-time activities.   30
[VI] Everyone carries round with him a fairly definite idea of the
primitive or natural conditions of human life. It is acquired more
by the study of humorous cartoons than of archaeology, but that
does not matter since it is not significant as theory but only as an
expression of inwardly felt expectations of people's sense of what   35
is fundamentally proper in the differentiation between the roles
of the two sexes. In this rudimentary natural society men go out
to hunt and fish and to fight off the tribe next door while women
keep the fire going. Amorous initiative is firmly reserved to the
man, who sets about courtship with a club.   40

B
[VII] This universal myth corresponds reasonably well to the way
duties have so far been divided between men and women in the
human enterprise. Woman's sphere of operations is the home,
while man's proving-ground is the great world outside. To the

extent that it is true that men are stronger, more aggressive (and　5
women more patient, more sensitive and gentler), this could be the
outcome of ordinary evolutionary selection. Men without the
characteristic male properties would not survive to reproduce
themselves; women without the characteristic properties of their
sex would fail to bring their children to maturity. Thus the　10
reproductively successful families would be those with highly
male fathers and highly female mothers.

[VIII] In considering the evidence it is reasonable to start in the
area with which feminists have always been most concerned:
work. Very few occupations are now exclusively confined to men:　15
mining, deep-sea fishing, the priesthood, violent crime (apart
from an occasional Bonnie), and its respectable counterpart, the
armed services. Two main problems, two main sources of distress
and friction, can be attributed to the increasing employment of
women. The first of these is that produced by the subordination　20
of men to women in hierarchical undertakings. There can be no
doubt that it takes a good deal of patience and self-control by
both parties when this situation comes about for the first time.
The woman may have to endanger her efficiency, and so give
ground for the inevitable doubts of her competence, by per-　25
suading where it would be much more convenient to command.
The man will have to forgo the kind of diluted amorousness
which is likely to be the habitual style of his relations with women
between sixteen and sixty.

[IX] The superior's inevitable task, from time to time, is to criti-　30
cize the work of subordinates. Unless criticism of men by women
takes' place within marriage, it is going to have an emotionally
disproportionate effect, to seem as much of an assault on the
male's potency as being overtaken on a motorway by a woman
driver. In fact this problem is still rather small. There are only　35
about a tenth as many women in jobs carrying salaries of £2000
a year or more as there should be if women had the share of top
jobs proportionate to their total working numbers.

C

[X] The other problem that arises from the employment of
women is that of the working wife. It has two aspects; that of the
wife who is more of a success than her husband and that of the
wife who must rely heavily on her husband for help with domestic
tasks. There are various ways in which the impact of the first　5
difficulty can be reduced. Provided that husband and wife are not

in the same or directly comparable lines of work the harsh fact
of her greater success can be obscured by a genial conspiracy
to reject a purely monetary measure of achievement as intolerably
crude. Where there are ranks, it is best if the couple work in 10
different fields so that the husband can find some special reason
for the superiority of the lowest figure in his to the most elevated in
his wife's.

[XI] A problem that affects a much larger number of working
wives is the need to re-allocate domestic tasks if there are children. 15
In *The Road to Wigan Pier* George Orwell wrote of the unem-
ployed of the Lancashire coalfields: 'Practically never . . . in a
working-class home, will you see the man doing a stroke of the
housework. Unemployment has not changed this convention,
which on the face of it seems a little unfair. The man is idle from 20
morning to night but the woman is as busy as ever—more so,
indeed, because she has to manage with less money. Yet so far as
my experience goes the women do not protest. They feel that a
man would lose his manhood if, merely because he was out of
work, he developed into a "Mary Ann".' 25

[XII] It is over the care of young children that this re-allocation of
duties becomes really significant. For this, unlike the cooking of
fish fingers or the making of beds, is an inescapably time-consum-
ing occupation, and time is what the fully employed wife has no
more to spare-of than her husband. 30

[XIII] The male initiative in courtship is a pretty indiscriminate
affair, something that is tried on with any remotely plausible
woman who comes within range and, of course, with all degrees
of tentativeness. What decides the issue of whether a genuine
courtship is going to get under way is the woman's response. If 35
she shows interest the engines of persuasion are set in movement.
The truth is that in courtship society gives women the real power
while pretending to give it to men.

[XIV] What does seem clear is that the more men and women are
together, at work and away from it, the more the comprehensive 40
amorousness of men towards women will have to go, despite all its
past evolutionary services. For it is this that makes inferiority at
work abrasive and, more indirectly, makes domestic work seem
unmanly. If there is to be an equalizing redistribution of economic and domestic tasks between men and women there must 45
be a compensating redistribution of the erotic initiative. If
women will no longer let us beat them they must allow us to join
them as the blushing recipients of flowers and chocolates.

ANTHONY QUINTON, *The Observer Colour Magazine*

After reading each of the following questions, choose the ONE correct answer, and indicate it by writing down the letter that stands for it. In all questions only ONE answer is correct. This is stressed in some questions, but remember that the rule applies to all of them.

From Section A

1 The opening quotation from Margaret Mead (ll. 1–6) sums up a relationship between man and woman which the writer

   A disapproves of
   B argues is natural
   C contrasts with the existing one
   D expects to go on changing
   E completely rejects

2 If we wanted to illustrate the truth of the same quotation which ONE of the following facts would we *not* quote?

   A women are not allowed to be bishops
   B few motoring offences are committed by women
   C few women commit crimes such as burglary
   D women are never (or rarely) stockbrokers
   E men, as well as women, are nurses

3 The phrase 'men's sureness of their sex role' (l. 3) suggests that they

   A are confident in their ability to charm women
   B take the initiative in courtship
   C have a clear idea of what is considered 'manly'
   D reserve the best careers for men
   E tend to be more immoral than women are

4 'Underwritten' (l. 5) means

   A preserved
   B emphasized
   C diluted
   D guaranteed
   E stressed

5 'Conclusion' (l. 7) means what Margaret Mead

   A continues her argument with
   B puts forward as a theory
   C decides is true
   D rejects as untenable
   E is reluctant to believe

6 The rest of the sentence from 'taking' (l. 15) to the end of the sentence in l. 19 describes

   A 'flow' (l. 12)
   B 'publications' (l. 12)

C 'bondage' (l. 12)
D 'advantages' (l. 14)
E 'defences' (l. 13)

7 Paragraph III does *not* claim that men
  A treat their wives like slaves in the home
  B prevent women from taking up certain professions
  C forbid women to join certain clubs and societies
  D doubt whether women really mean to succeed in business
  E secretly admire women's intellect and resolution

8 Which ONE of the following is used literally, *not* metaphorically?
  A 'tied up with' (l. 3)
  B 'flow' (l. 12)
  C 'thrown up' (l. 14)
  D 'erosion' (l. 21)
  E 'approximation' (l. 27–8)

9 Paragraph III
  A generally agrees with the first paragraph
  B has no connection with the first paragraph
  C generally agrees with the fifth paragraph
  D contradicts the sixth paragraph
  E repeats the argument of the previous (second) paragraph

10 At the end of paragraph VI the writer uses humorous exaggeration in order to
  A underline his point
  B disown the ideas he is expressing
  C show that men are stronger than women
  D carry further the ideas of earlier paragraphs
  E help us to believe the idea of the first sentence of the same paragraph

11 The usual idea of the cave man (paragraph VI)
  A is based on the study of archaeology
  B is significant as a theory about prehistoric times
  C illustrates how people expect men to behave
  D proves that the man, not woman, should be the wooer
  E is dismissed by this writer as an irrelevant joke

12 This writer is using 'natural' (l. 37) in the sense of
  A uncivilized
  B charitable
  C instinctive
  D unsophisticated
  E elementary

From Section B

13 Which ONE of the following words shows that the writer does *not* completely accept the ideas of paragraph VII?

    A 'universal' (l. 1)
    B 'myth' (l. 1)
    C 'corresponds' (l. 1)
    D 'duties' (l. 2)
    E 'divided' (l. 2)

14 Which of the following functions are performed by paragraph VIII?

    i it turns its back on the past
    ii it considers social changes that have already begun
    iii it refers to problems created by those changes
    iv it deals with different ideas from those of paragraphs I, II, VI and VII
    v its later ideas are results of its first idea

Which ONE of the following gives the correct functions?

    A i, ii and iii
    B i, iii and v
    C i, ii, iii and v
    D i, ii, iv and v
    E all of them

15 'Give ground for' (l. 24) means

    A surrender to
    B provide justification for
    C make concessions to
    D create opportunities for
    E take notice of

16 'The man . . . between sixteen and sixty' (ll. 27–9) means that men will

    A have to adopt a stricter code of morality
    B inevitably half-fall in love with many women
    C have to stop flirting with women they meet at work
    D inevitably feel attracted to women of different ages
    E deny that they are naturally polygamous

17 'Hierarchical undertakings' (l. 21) are those where workers

    A co-operate with one another
    B are drawn from both sexes
    C are placed in ranks above and below each other
    D adopt a semi-military structure
    E are dominated by class consciousness

18 'Inevitable' (l. 30) means

    A unpleasant
    B essential
    C unavoidable
    D inherent
    E specific

From Section C

19 Paragraph X advises the working wife who is more successful than her husband to

    A put her family before her career
    B work in the same sort of job as her husband
    C play down her success, making it sound unimportant
    D stress how much the family gains from her high salary
    E introduce more labour-saving machinery into the home

20 Orwell's picture of relations between man and wife in Wigan (paragraph XI) describes a relationship which the author

    A thinks is the natural one
    B wishes to see preserved
    C is ridiculing as comically absurd
    D is sure must change
    E thinks is fair

21 Which ONE of the following words is used literally, *not* metaphorically?

    A 'heavily' (l. 4)
    B 'fields' (l. 11)
    C 'engines' (l. 36)
    D 'convention' (l. 37)
    E 'abrasive' (l. 43)

22 'Genial' (l. 8) means

    A untruthful
    B kindly
    C innocent
    D sociable
    E family

23 Paragraph XIV stresses that if women are to hold important jobs, then they must

    A not criticize their male subordinates at work
    B be tactful and not make their husbands seem 'Mary Anns'
    C sometimes make the first advances in love
    D allow men to flirt with many women
    E stop accepting presents of flowers and chocolates

24 Which of the following statements does the article make about the present form of courtship?

    i each man 'makes passes' at many women
    ii some of these are more serious than others
    iii the man leaves himself the opportunity to give up the chase quickly
    iv the woman's reaction to his first advance decides whether he continues it
    v society does not admit the truth that the woman can determine how far the courtship goes

Which ONE of the following gives the correct statements?

A i, ii and iii
B i, ii, iii and iv
C i, ii, iii and v
D i, ii, iv and v
E all of them

From the Whole Passage

25 A suitable title for the whole passage would be

A Continuing changes in the roles of women
B Ought wives to work?
C All husbands want to be cave men
D The male's idea of manliness
E Sex inequalities that persist

26 The article gives specific consideration to working-class men in paragraph(s)

A VI, VII and VIII
B VII and XI
C XI
D I and VII
E VII and X

Additional Question
[*Time allowed: 1 hour*]

27 a In 80 of your own words explain the social roles that men have played in this country.
    b In 80 of your own words explain what progress **i** has occurred, and **ii** has not occurred, in the emancipation of women.
    c Identify, and comment on, passages in which the writer describes relationships between men and women that belong to the past, not the present.

Paper 11

Part One

[Time allowed: 1 hour for question 1; 30 minutes for question 2]

1 Write a composition on *one* of the following subjects:
  a Suppose you were writing an account of your childhood in such a way as to emphasize your relations with your family. Write a few pages that might form part of such a book.
  b My family at a meal.
  c The transport problems of your country or district and how they could be solved.
  d Baby-sitting.
  e Suppose that you have been looking forward for a long time to some special event that directly concerns you. The outcome is disappointing. Write about the feelings you have had before the event, while it was taking place, and now that it is all over.
  f The following are quotations from speeches or from letters to newspapers. Give your opinion on *one* of them.
    i If we allow everyone who wants to quarry chalk or gravel in beauty spots to do so, then the beauty of England will be destroyed, and it will become a series of huge gravel-pits connected by motorways.
    ii If the members of the League against Cruel Sports get their way, they will turn us all into vegetarians. They are nothing but fanatics. Wild-fowling is just one of the innocent pleasures that they wish to deny us.
    iii Considering the economic situation of Britain, what justification is there for the government's proposal to purchase a jet plane for the Prime Minister's use at a cost of £370 000? What's wrong with British Rail?

2 *Either*
  a Write a letter to your local newspaper in reply to a letter published in it criticizing *one* of the following:
    school trips abroad; the study of a particular school subject; your favourite television programme; recent rises in prices.
  Or
  b Describe the most striking poster or T.V. advertisement you have ever seen, explaining how the designer attracted your attention.

Part Two
[*Time allowed: 1 hour*]

Read the following passage and then answer the questions.

I am not interested here in the argument whether there should be
zoos, but in how to make them better. Nevertheless, I should
perhaps state that I welcome zoos, just as I welcome museums and
art galleries, as show-cases of creation. I do not think animals
should live only in their countries of origin, and I believe zoos   5
have a part to play both in keeping animals alive and in keeping
interest in them alive. To send a tiger back to India is both to
forget about the species and to kill that individual. India's tiger
population is now about 1600, is shrinking rapidly (and reasonably, for large wild carnivores are difficult cohabitants) and may   10
shrink to extinction. Already there are more tigers outside India
than in it. They are mainly in zoos, and these will keep them safe.

It is therefore desirable that zoos keep their animals alive (to
save dipping again into the shrinking reservoir of wild life), that
these animals should breed, that the zoo's visitors can both see   15
the exhibits and be interested by them. The traditional picture of
a zoo cage, carried in the minds of so many of us, satisfies none of
these conditions. The animal is frequently short-lived, and
obviously bored, unwell or lifeless during its mismanaged
existence. It is not breeding for the most elementary reason of   20
all—that it has no mate. It is probably huddled in a corner, and
neither stimulates, interests nor delights us. We prod it with a
stick or throw a stone to get our money's worth. A snarl will do.

In the beginning, when zoos were new, it was enough to show
off one wild beast in a cage. Think of the excitement when   25
London's first giraffes walked from Tilbury to Regent's Park.
Where else could an illiterate majority or even the literate
minority see such creatures? The zoo sights were tremendous.
London's famous elephant Jumbo even gave his name to anything monstrously big. 'Walking in the zoo, it's the OK thing to   30
do' they sang back in 1877, and the Zoological Society of London
was the first place in the world to be abbreviated into a 'zoo'.

Today they still sing:

> Happy birthday to you,
> I went to the Zoo,   35
> And I saw a fat monkey
> Who looked exactly like you.

But the visitors are now less satisfied with stodgy animals in poor surroundings. People are now literate. They have travelled more. They have watched the very best nature films on television, 40 showing penguins leaping from Antarctic seas, gibbons brachiating through the tree-tops, wildebeest thundering over the Serengeti. They complain if the reality of the zoo does not match up to their hopes, if the penguins, gibbons and wildebeest are standing on concrete: static, useless, pointless. They want more 45 for their higher entrance charges.

In making the BBC-2 series 'Great Zoos of the World' we visited the zoos of San Diego, Tucson, Antwerp, Hamburg, West Berlin, Frankfurt, Basle and London. We could well have added another twenty or thirty to this reconnaissance list, and then 50 made our selection, but budgets and time do not allow such luxuries. As it was, we chose to include all the zoos we visited except Hamburg, which was unfair because Hamburg really started the modern zoo. What it did at the start of this century some zoos have now done and all ought to have done. Having 55 first learnt the jumping distance of its animals, Hamburg tried to do away with the cage. Instead of bars they put barriers of dry moats and wet ones, of small walls or bushes, and for the cage they had mountains and hillocks fashioned from false rock or real rock. Anything, they felt, was better than the ordinary prison. 60

London then built its Mappin terraces, another early triumph of condensed zoo-keeping. However, in any old zoo, building something new means knocking something else down, and legacies are often hard to remove. San Diego started its world-famous zoo about a century later than the big European cities 65 had done, and had no hideous left-overs of imperial architecture, no Greek temples reborn as aquariums, no caryatids holding up monkey houses. In all zoos, with new ideas so quickly becoming old, it emphatically pays to have as little of the past as possible. 'Why,' said Dr. Bernhard Grzimek of Frankfurt Zoo to Prince 70 Philip, 'could our air forces not have co-operated? We could have bombed yours, and you could have bombed ours.' We 'co-operated' more than they did, and Frankfurt and Berlin now have new zoos. London is still lumbered with much of its old one.

Part of San Diego's excellence is that it is obsessed with 75 modernity. In standard American fashion, it will tear anything down, even the following year, if the animals have shown it to be unsatisfactory. They never build for posterity, but for next year, and possibly for a few more years if it is good. 'Very old' to them

is anything in its twenties. When one zoo develops a good idea 80
all the old ideas for that species suddenly look as antiquated as a
Victorian underground system or parental fashions. Think of
tigers without a place to swim in, polar bears not being able to
dive, penguins having no ice to stand on, large birds not being
able to fly, herd animals not in groups, flamingoes not making 85
nests of mud, animals being alone.

The rise of breeding is the most important zoo event. Basle are
pre-eminent at it. They consider it indecent to have a single
animal, and would rather give it away if a suitable mate could be
found elsewhere. Ninety-nine per cent of zoos spend more on 90
buying animals than they receive for selling them. Basle spends
S.Frs 5000 a year on purchases, but gets 90 000 from sales. It has
bred 41 pygmy hippos, 11 Indian rhinos, 4 Lowland gorillas, and
its solitary post-war pair of Bengal tigers now have great-great-
grandchildren. It should have been axiomatic right from the start 95
that Chi-Chi and An-An got together, and China—whose Peking
Zoo has bred giant pandas—should have given advice. The zoos
are being bullied from every angle to think more about breeding.
The public likes to see young creatures. Many animals do better
if breeding. Some traditional supplies from the wild are drying 100
up. Some are cut off by law. (No horse—which includes zebras—
can be imported into Europe from Africa because of horse
sickness.) Zoos prefer to buy zoo-reared animals rather than the
dubious, frightened, diseased purchases from their natural
habitat. And, as Basle has shown, it is profitable to breed and sell 105
the produce.

'What makes a good zoo?' I asked Dr. Ralph Schroeder, head
of San Diego. 'Dollars,' he said. Yet his zoo might seem at first to
be making every effort not to acquire more. All children, service-
men and teachers get in free, and San Diego city consists almost 110
entirely of the US Navy and huge families. Instead, the whole
zoo is dotted with efficient, desirable, hot and cold slot-machines
which work. There is also a sky-chair ride to the other side:
'Gee, mom, please . . .' So San Diego gets its money.

Many zoos, uncertain of their educational status, think 115
blatant money-making is indecent. Various entrepreneurs,
skilled cash-spinners elsewhere, would love to get their hands on
city zoos. The Longleat lions, now added to by more than a dozen
other species, are making a fortune for their masters, while London Zoo and Whipsnade are finding it hard to make ends meet. 120
In my opinion you can smell whether a zoo is making money the

moment you walk into it. And the public, fickle, casual and disloyal, is always happiest to give its support and money to the already profitable.

The best zoos seem to have dictators at their head. Klös of 125 Berlin says he has no trouble with architects wanting to build monuments; he fires them. Schroeder throws down some litter, and waits in the shadows to watch it picked up. 'Here it may take twenty minutes. At Disneyland it takes five.' Grzimek practically tells the German public on television what animals to be interested 130 in this month, and he certainly tells them not to wear leopard-skin coats. Lang of Basle is the man behind his zoo's formidable obstetric success. 'When I came we had one gorilla. What is the use of one gorilla?' Two of Britain's best provincial zoos, Bristol and Chester, have positive, efficient and single-minded men in 135 charge of them.

Is a zoo for entertainment or education? Antwerp says educa-tion. San Diego says entertain them first and then wham into them with some education. Most zoos oscillate, and put up incredibly learned descriptions of a species when the pertinent 140 questions might be: 'Why is it standing on one leg?' 'Does it sting with its tongue?' 'Why is its bottom all red?' Zoos often say they are museums. The state only rarely says so, because most museums and art galleries are wholly subsidized, while all zoos are expected to be self-supporting, or largely so. Zoos say they are 145 not circuses, but admit that many animals and birds will put on an act with little provocation and scarcely any training. Think of chimpanzees, sea-lions, elephants, mynahs.

ANTHONY SMITH, 'Zoos' (The Listener)

After reading each of the following questions, choose the ONE correct answer, and indicate it by writing down the letter that stands for it. In all questions only ONE answer is correct. This is stressed in some questions, but remember that the rule applies to all of them.

1 'Carnivores' (l. 10) are

  A large mammals

  B man-eaters

  C insect-eating plants

  D flesh-eating animals or plants

  E eaters of carrion

2 The writer says that he

   i approves of the existence of zoos

   ii wants to improve zoos

   iii does not like animals being kept outside their own countries in zoos

   iv believes zoos save certain animals from extinction

   v believes zoos help to keep people interested in animals

Which ONE of the following gives the correct statements?

A i, iii and iv

B i, ii, iii and iv .

C ii, iv and v.

D iii, iv and v

E i, ii, iv and v

3 The words inside the brackets in ll. 13–14 compare the capture of a wild animal to

A revisiting a lake

B drying up a shallow lake

C emptying a water supply

D taking water from a declining source ·

E burning one's seed corn

4 The purpose of the dash in l. 21 is that it

A isolates what follows

B prepares the reader for a joke

C admits the grammatical incompleteness of the sentence

D introduces a descriptive clause

E breaks the sentence up into two parts

5 In early zoos animals

   i did not live long

   ii lived monotonous lives

   iii were cruelly treated by visitors

   iv did not breed

   v were usually kept in cages

Which ONE of the following gives the correct statements?

A i, ii, iii and iv

B i, ii, iv and v

C ii, iii and iv

D ii, iv and v

E all of them

6 The ONE of the following statements that is *not* true is

  A the reader is intended to be surprised by the sentence 'Already . . . . . it' (l. 11)

  B the writer implies that it is cruel to throw a stone at an animal

  C it was easy for the London Zoo to thrill visitors in its early years

  D the grammar of ll. 31–2 is deliberately odd: a society (as distinct from its name) cannot be abbreviated

  E the writer makes ironic fun of what he calls 'the very best nature films' (l. 40)

7 Visitors to zoos are dissatisfied with animals in poor surroundings for all the following reasons *except* for the ONE reason that they

  A have travelled more

  B are able to read and write

  C have watched films of animals in natural surroundings

  D have paid more to go in

  E wish to abolish zoos altogether

8 Television has made visitors to zoos

  A more easily bored

  B more demanding

  C better informed

  D more interested

  E willing to pay more

9 'Reconnaissance list' (l. 50) means a list for

  A spying

  B a preliminary survey

  C inspection

  D a sample inquiry

  E an examination

10 It was unfair *not* to include Hamburg Zoo in the BBC programmes because

  A Hamburg Zoo was very well known

  B Hamburg Zoo was the first of a new type of zoo

  C in Hamburg Zoo natural surroundings were replacing cages

  D in Hamburg Zoo animals were able to jump over moats

  E in Hamburg Zoo cages were made of concrete

11 The main reason why it pays to have as little of the past as possible in zoos is that

  A new ideas are quickly superseded

  B moats are preferable to false rock

  C such work can only be paid for by legacies

  D imperial architecture is hideous

  E Greek temples do not hold water

12 'They never build for posterity' (l. 78) means they
    A build only for succeeding generations
    B build chiefly for the present
    C build for their ancestors
    D build as cheaply as possible
    E never build to commemorate

13 Which ONE of the following is *not* stressed in this article as a reason for zoos to concentrate on breeding?
    A they can no longer buy some wild animals
    B some animals are not allowed to be imported
    C people are interested in young animals
    D many animals are healthier if breeding
    E zoo-reared animals are tame

14 In the context of the word, 'legacies' (l. 63) compares
    A the effect of the past to money left in wills
    B traditions to bequests
    C inherited buildings in zoos to estate duties
    D old buildings to inherited wealth
    E consequences of the past to present-day survivors

15 Dr. Bernhard Grzimek suggested that the British and German air forces should have
    A both bombed each other's zoos
    B worked together for peaceful ends
    C been used to collect wild animals
    D been used to destroy old zoological buildings
    E appreciated the freedom of wild beasts in natural surroundings

16 'Skilled cash-spinners' (l. 117) means
    A good spenders
    B efficient money-makers
    C trained performers
    D expert financiers
    E skilful bankers

17 Which ONE of the following expressions is used literally *not* metaphorically?
    A 'reservoir' (l. 14)
    B 'reborn' (l. 67)
    C 'are drying up' (l. 100)
    D 'are making a bomb' (l. 119)
    E 'litter' (l. 127)

18 An 'obstetric success' (l. 133) is a success in

   A making money
   B breeding young animals
   C attracting visitors
   D providing entertainment
   E educating visitors

19 In its particular context in l. 139 to 'oscillate' means to

   A coincide
   B keep changing one's mind
   C go up and down
   D change one's mind
   E alternate

20 The state rarely calls zoos 'museums' because

   A the exhibits in museums are not alive
   B the animals in museums are stuffed
   C zoos are expected to be self-supporting
   D zoos are privately owned
   E zoos are not unlike circuses

Additional Question
[*Time allowed: 30 minutes*]

21 a Explain the meaning of *two* of the following:
    i 'budgets and time do not allow such luxuries' (l. 51)
    ii 'it is obsessed with modernity' (l. 75)
    iii 'uncertain of their educational status' (l. 115)
  b How does the San Diego Zoo finance itself?

Paper 12

Part One

[*Time allowed: 1 hour for question 1 ; 30 minutes for question 2*]

1 Write a composition on *one* of the following subjects:
   a The persistent disadvantages of being a woman.
   b The advantages and disadvantages of being an only child.
   c The scene and setting and crowd before the beginning of an important game or sports meeting.
   d A family outing.
   e Superstition in our lives today.
   f The pleasures of collecting.
   g 'No warmth, no cheerfulness, no healthful ease,
   No shade, no shine, no butterflies, no bees,
   No fruits, no flowers, no leaves, no trees
   November!'
   What are your impressions of this month?
   h The good and bad effects of speed.

2 *Either*
   a Write a persuasive letter, giving details about an article that you have advertised for sale, in answer to a letter of inquiry. Invent suitable details.
   Or
   b Give clear instructions on how to do *one* of the following well:
   erect a garden fence; service a motor-cycle or scooter; paint a room; make a dress; change a car wheel; make an omelette; rescue a drowning person.

Part Two

[*Time allowed: 1 hour*]

Read the following passage (which for your convenience has been divided into two sections) and then answer the questions.

[A] The Civic Trust has pointed out: 'Beauty has an economic value, ugliness has an economic cost.' A study group at the 1965 Conference of the Countryside in 1970 concluded: 'The control of

dereliction should be recognized as being of equal social consequence as other forms of environmental control: clean streets, 5
clean air and clean rivers.' Perhaps both these bodies were too far
out-pacing 'public opinion' and government thinking.

John Oxenham, formerly the official adviser on land reclamation to the Ministry of Housing and Local Government, has said
in his authoritative book *Reclaiming Derelict Land*: 'Cost has 10
always been held up as the deterrent to every social improvement.'
He cited Acts of Parliament requiring clean water, sewerage,
clean air—all of them delayed not for decades but for centuries
beyond the recognition of the evils they finally attacked. And
today—though industrial dereliction may be recognized as an 15
evil—'it will cost too much . . . . we just can't afford it' is the
frequent response at all levels of government to suggestions
that a determined, military operation be started to restore or
landscape at least the hard core of dereliction left from the
industrial revolution—the 80 000 or so acres in Britain which the 20
government itself considers to 'justify treatment'. Britain's
current economic difficulties are of course frequently cited,
because they are a strong argument for doing nothing. Yet it is all
too apparent that the economic squeeze is a convenient pretext
for a government which really doesn't want to act, and a pretext 25
positively welcomed by many apathetic local authorities who
simply don't want to know about the problem of dereliction.

Estimates of how much a ten-year reclamation programme of
the worst of the existing dereliction would cost range from £20
million to £60 million: about £35 million is now a widely accepted 30
figure, based on the costs incurred by a few enlightened authorities, such as Lancashire, which have gone ahead with land
renewal despite the lack of incentives. This works out at little
more than a shilling per head of population per year. Can we not
afford this amount to rehabilitate our environment? Perhaps one 35
trouble is that industrial dereliction is a gradual, insidious
degradation; when a sudden, brutal attack on this beautiful
island occurs—such as the *Torrey Canyon* oil-tanker disaster in
1967—millions are somehow produced overnight to save the
nation from despoliation. Can we not afford £34 million over 40
ten years? This nation of gardeners spends about that amount
each year on seeds, plants, shrubs, ornamental trees—on things
to enhance the *private* environment. This nation of pet-keepers
spends nearly that amount *each year* on pet accessories—feeding
bowls, dog beds, catnip mice, budgie toys—designed to improve 45

the environment of our thirteen million cats, dogs and caged birds.

The question too seldom asked is: 'What is it costing us *not* to renew our dead lands?' That is the proper question. The answers are so apparent that it makes our inaction all the more disgraceful.   50

[B] First of all, industrial wastelands are a visual affront. They offend the eye, they offend what is one of the world's most civilized landscapes. More than thirty years ago Thomas Sharp wrote: 'A landscape is an index to a civilization.' To tolerate dereliction spattering that landscape, to expect people to live   5
amidst dereliction, is not civilized.

Derelict land, and the industrial junk left behind when industry has made its profit and fled, is dangerous to life. Robert Howard, M.P. for Bolton East, raised this point during an adjournment debate (on derelict sites) in the Commons in April 1967. He   10
cited examples of children killed in abandoned cotton mills, drowned in disused canals or while playing on frozen flashes, the treacherous ponds that collect on ground subsided from mining. In Bolton in April 1968 three girls and a fireman coming to their rescue were killed by gas accumulated in a disused colliery. It was   15
not the Coal Board's fault, but it pointed up the constant danger to life of the tens of thousands of sealed mine entrances in the country. In 1968, according to the Royal Society for the Prevention of Accidents, there were 227 accidental deaths in Great Britain in mines and quarries, including seventeen children under   20
fifteen years of age, eleven of whom drowned. Not all of those children died necessarily in *derelict* mines and quarries, but it can be assumed that a majority did.

Derelict land—and the assorted rubbish which its ugliness and uselessness attracts—is dangerous to health. The British Ecolo-   25
gical Society has pointed out that reclamation is sometimes required not for commercial or recreational reasons but simply on public health grounds, to eliminate flies and vermin and to remove the nuisance of dust. At the 1967 annual conference of the Association of Public Health Inspectors, John Stephenson noted   30
sorrowfully: 'The easiest and cheapest way to dispose of refuse is to find a large hole in the ground, empty the rubbish into it and beat a hasty retreat.' This method of crude tipping was still used in 1967 by no fewer than 115 local authorities, and another 460 authorities got rid of their rubbish by 'semi-controlled' tipping,   35
often little better. While thoroughly controlled tipping of town

refuse can make a valuable contribution to land reclamatión, these primitive methods only further aggravate already repulsive dereliction and create public health problems. Dereliction is a magnet for more dereliction.

Derelict land, in an age of rising aspirations and growing demands for a better environment, contributes to depopulation, to the migration—particularly of the young—to areas less debased by industrial mess. And much of the nation's dereliction is in the development areas or 'grey' districts of northern England and Wales, the very places to which the government is attempting to entice people. A 1968 study of dereliction in the West Riding by the county planning department has established a correlation between outward migration from districts of high spoliation and inward migration to areas of low spoliation, especially among young females. John Casson, the county's deputy planning officer, believes TV advertising and films are setting new, materialistically higher physical standards and that young people in drab old areas of the country increasingly seek those higher standards elsewhere. He also raises a point often lost sight of by planners in Whitehall: 'By leaving the dereliction here (and so contributing to outward migration) we are escalating the pressures on, say, Buckinghamshire.'

Derelict land, and the wider degraded environment of which it is so often a part and to which it contributes, is a deterrent to modern industry. Top executives—and even more, perhaps, their wives—are much more reluctant than trees or grass to put down their roots in shale heaps and arsenical soil. Casson and L. A. King, West Riding's forestry officer, told the British Association for the Advancement of Science at its 1967 conference: 'The most powerful stimulus to the flow of capital under modern conditions is first-class environment . . . . without environment renewal the North may be condemned to increasing dependence on the older and declining staple industries.' In County Durham, Richard Atkinson has found: 'Industrialists are increasingly critical of the environment in which they choose to establish new projects, and potential industrial developments have been lost from parts (of Durham) simply because the quality of town or landscape was not good enough for them.'

JOHN BARR, *Derelict Britain* (Penguin)

After reading each of the following questions, choose the ONE correct answer, and indicate it by writing down the letter that stands for it. In all questions only ONE answer is correct. This is stressed in some questions, but remember that the rule applies to all of them.

From Section A

1 'Dereliction' (l. 4) refers to land that

    A has been ruined and misused
    B offends our love of beauty
    C is on the outskirts of industrial areas
    D has ceased to be used productively
    E is no longer used for farming

2 'Consequence' (l. 4) means

    A result
    B importance
    C rank
    D status
    E outcome

3 The Civic Trust and the 1965 Conference of the Countryside in 1970

    A had great influence on people's ideas
    B had great influence on government policy
    C were in advance of the ideas of the people and the government
    D lagged behind public opinion
    E deliberately flouted public opinion

4 'Cost has always been held up as the deterrent to every social improvement' (ll. 10–11) means that social improvement

    A is always inevitably costly
    B is always inexpensive in taxpayers' eyes
    C cannot be stopped by lack of money
    D has always been hindered by the consideration of expense
    E can never be too costly

5 'Cited' (l. 12) means

    A memorized
    B recited
    C recalled
    D produced
    E instanced

6 Which ONE of the following is used literally, *not* metaphorically?

    A 'out-pacing' (l. 7)
    B 'military' (l. 18)
    C 'hard core' (l. 19)

D 'squeeze' (l. 24)
E 'apathetic' (l. 26)

7 'Pretext' (l. 24) means

A excuse
B reason
C pretence
D evasion
E white lie

8 Little land is being reclaimed because

    i the government claims that the cost would be prohibitive
    ii some local authorities have no interest
    iii industrial spoiling of land is gradual and unnoticed
    iv too much is spent on private gardens
    v clean land is less important than clean water and clean air

Which ONE of the following gives the correct reasons?

A i, ii, iv and v
B ii, iv and v
C i, iii and v
D i, ii and iii
E ii, iii, iv and v

9 'Enhance' (l. 43) means

A increase
B improve
C invigorate
D correct
E reform

10 'Apathetic' (l. 26) means

A indifferent
B unenlightened
C disinterested
D miserly
E insensitive

From Section B

11 'Index' (l. 4) means

A a pointer to the existence of
B a method of evaluating
C an example of
D a useful symbol of
E a symptom of the illness of

12 'Aggravate' (l. 38) means

    A exaggerate
    B make worse
    C make exasperating
    D contaminate
    E provoke

13 Which ONE of the following is used literally, *not* metaphorically?

    A 'spattering' (l. 5)
    B 'magnet' (l. 40)
    C 'correlation' (l. 48)
    D 'escalating' (l. 57)
    E 'put down their roots' (l. 62)

14 In its particular context in l. 22 'Necessarily' means

    A because society lacked the means to prevent it
    B it must be deduced
    C from lack of playing facilities
    D because the cost of closing derelict mines and quarries is prohibitive
    E because of lack of rescue organizations

15 There is a deliberate element of repetition in each of the following pairs of words with the ONE EXCEPTION of

    A 'affront' . . . . . . 'offend' (ll. 1–2)
    B 'commercial' . . . . . . 'recreational' (l. 27)
    C 'derelict' . . . . . . 'junk' (l. 7)
    D 'abandoned' . . . . . . 'disused' (ll. 11–12)
    E 'refuse' . . . . . . 'rubbish' (ll. 31–2)

16 Which ONE of the following statements about metaphors is *not* true?

    A 'industrial wastelands' (l. 1) are said to insult our eyes and our scenery
    B industry that uses an area (l. 7) and then abandons it leaves behind the equivalent of useless belongings
    C an evil human quality is attributed to ponds (l. 13)
    D in l. 28 flies attracted to rubbish tips are compared to rats and mice
    E in ll. 31–3 those who tip rubbish into holes are compared to an army running away

17 The fact that some areas of northern England are made ugly by dereliction has each one of the following results *except* that it

    A tempts some towns to dump rubbish in an unsightly, unhealthy manner
    B drives many young people to leave the district
    C thwarts the government's attempts to attract new industry to these areas

D seems to affect the whole of the West Riding alike
E increases over-population in pleasant counties fairly near London

From the Whole Passage

18 The author does *not* regard the individuals whose opinions he quotes as

   A comparatively wise and far-sighted
   B bravely and intelligently ahead of public opinion
   C more enlightened than the government
   D unrealistic in ignoring the cost of reclamation
   E regretful of how much derelict land persists

19 Which of the following arguments does the article advance for controlling dereliction?

   i dereliction causes pollution of air and rivers
   ii dereliction spoils the appearance of our naturally lovely landscapes
   iii dereliction is unenlightened and uncivilized
   iv dereliction prevents a proper distribution of population throughout the country
   v dereliction encourages unhealthy methods of tipping

Which ONE of the following gives the correct arguments?

   A i, ii and iii
   B ii, iii, iv and v
   C i, ii, iii and v
   D i, iii, iv and v
   E all of them

20 The most suitable title for this passage would be

   A The Aberfans of northern England
   B Why more derelict land must be reclaimed
   C The economic costs of dereliction
   D The brass has gone; the muck remains
   E Beauty has an economic value

Additional Question

21 a Summarize in about 100 of your own words the effects of derelict land on the community.
   b What are the economic arguments for and against reclaiming derelict land?

Paper 13

Part One

[Time allowed: 1 hour for question 1; 30 minutes for question 2]

1 Write a composition on *one* of the following subjects:

  a Discuss the reasons why many people today read books about *either* the First World War *or* the Second World War.

  b Write a description of the dispersal of a crowd such as might form part of a novel.

  c Uncles.

  d Write about recent attempts by man to harness the forces of nature.

  e The changes you have noticed in yourself over the last five years.

  f Do games make people friendlier?

  g Write about what *one* of the following quotations suggests to you:

    i 'At this village, religious as a psalm,
    peaceful by this English river's edge,
    light visits the undersides of bridges,
    midges dare the olive water's calm.'

    ii 'Not till about
    One-twenty of the sunlit Saturday
    Did my three-quarters-empty train pull out,
    All windows down, all cushions hot, all sense
    Of being in a hurry gone. We ran
    Behind the backs of houses, crossed a street
    Of blinding windscreens, smelt the fish-dock.'

    iii 'The hero was
    A milky wide-brimmed hat, a shape
    Astride the arched white stallion;
    The villain's horse and hat were black.
    Disbelief did not exist
    And laundered virtue always won
    With quicker gun and harder fist,
    And all of us applauded it.'

2 *Either*

  a Describe clearly *one* of the following and explain how it is used:
    a typewriter; a film projector; an electric sewing-machine; a record-player; the carburettor of a motor-car.

Or

b Write a clear and factual report for the police of an accident that
you have witnessed.

Part Two

[*Time allowed: 1 hour*]

Read the following passage and then answer the questions.

The gorilla is something of a paradox in the African scene. One
thinks one knows him well. For a hundred years or more he has
been killed, captured and imprisoned in zoos. His bones have
been mounted in natural history museums everywhere, and he
has always exerted a strong fascination upon scientists and   5
romantics alike. He is the stereotyped monster of the horror
films and the adventure books, and an obvious (though not
perhaps strictly scientific) link with our ancestral past.

Yet the fact is we know very little about gorillas. No really
satisfactory photograph has ever been taken of one in a wild   10
state; no zoologist, however intrepid, has been able to keep the
animal under close and constant observation in the dark jungles
in which it lives. Carl Akeley, the American naturalist, led two
expeditions to Uganda in the 1920's and now lies buried there
among the animals he loved so well; but even he was unable to   15
discover how long the gorilla lives, or how or why it dies, nor was
he able to define the exact social pattern of the family groups, or
indicate the final extent of their intelligence. All this and many
other things remain almost as much a mystery as they were when
the French explorer Du Chaillu first described the animal to the   20
civilized world a century ago. The Abominable Snowman who
haunts the imagination of climbers in the Himalayas is hardly
more elusive.

The little that is known about gorillas certainly makes you
want to know more. Sir Julian Huxley has recorded that thrice in   25
the London Zoo he saw an eighteen-month-old specimen trace
the outline of its own shadow with its finger. 'No similar artistic
initiative,' he writes, 'has been recorded for any other anthropoid,
though we all know now that young chimpanzees will paint
"pictures" if provided with the necessary materials.' Huxley   30
speaks too of a traveller seeing a male gorilla help a female up a
steep rock-step, and gallantry of that kind is certainly not
normal among animals. It is this 'human-ness' of the gorilla that

is so beguiling. According to some observers he courts and makes
love in the same way as humans do. Once the family is established   35
it clings together. It feeds in a group in the thick bamboo jungles
on the mountainside in the daytime, each animal making a tidy
pile of its food—wild celery, bamboo shoots, and other leaves—
and squatting down to eat it; and by night each member of the
family makes its own bed by bending over and interlacing the   40
bamboo fronds so as to form a kind of oval-shaped nest which is
as comfortable and springy as a mattress. The father tends to
make his bed just a foot or two from the ground, the mother a
little higher, and the children are safely lodged in the branches up
above.   45

When he walks the gorilla takes the main weight on his short
legs and rests lightly on the knuckles of his hands at the end of his
very long arms. When he stands upright a full-grown male rises
to six feet, but with that immense chest he is far heavier than any
normal man could ever be. Six hundred pounds is not uncommon.   50
His strength is incredible—certainly great enough to take a man
in his arms and wrench his head off.

Gorillas appear to talk to one another in high-pitched voices,
not unlike those of women, or by smacking their lips or striking
their cheeks, and the female, if alarmed, will scream. The male is   55
capable of making a frightening demonstration in the face of
danger. He stays behind while his family gets away, rising to his
feet and uttering a terrifying roar. Sometimes he will drum on his
chest and shake the trees around him with every appearance of
uncontrollable fury. In extremity he will charge.   60

But all this is no more than shadow boxing as a general rule,
for the gorilla is a gentle, kindly creature, a most forgiving ape
who lives at peace with all the other animals, and his reputation
for savagery and belligerence is nothing but a myth. When the
animal charges, the thing to do is to stand your ground and look   65
him in the eye. Then he will turn aside and slip away through the
undergrowth.

ALAN MOOREHEAD, *No Room in the Ark*
(Hamish Hamilton and Laurence Pollinger Ltd)

1 In about 90 words explain what are the main facts about gorillas that
mankind **a** knows, **b** does not know.

2 In about 80 words explain the main ways in which gorillas resemble
humans.

3 Explain what a paradox is and explain briefly why the author calls the gorilla 'a paradox'.

4 Choose any one paragraph and analyse it in such a way as to show that the author views gorillas sympathetically and is resolved to think the best of them.

Part Three

[*Time allowed: 1 hour*]

Read the following passage (which for your convenience has been divided into three sections) and then answer the questions.

[A] For over fifty years, from 1154 to 1216, England was ruled by a man from Anjou in France and two of his sons. They were King Henry II, King Richard I, and King John.

These Angevin rulers of England had marked characteristics of personality. They were passionate and dynamic, with clever   5
minds and strong wills. They had a hot temper which sometimes prejudiced their calculated schemes. They seemed, even to contemporaries, a little larger than life. Their minds and bodies appeared to work faster than those of normal men. When they conceived anything it was usually on a grand scale; their will   10
matched their conception, and their vast resources were bent to its realization. Henry II was 'a human chariot' drawing every thing after him. He never seemed to take a moment's rest: in church even he scribbled or drew pictures; while hearing matters of business he would be mending his hunting gear; in relaxation   15
he would hunt from dawn until sunset, pushing through woods and mountain passes, and even then weary his court after supper by remaining on his feet. To be in his household was to know the fury of Hell, said his courtiers. Richard I, differing from his father in build and colouring and in his zest for war, was like him   20
in a ruthless energy that brooked no opposition: the builders of his castle at Les Andelys were startled one day by a shower of blood, but the king forced them on, 'and even if an angel had descended from heaven to urge its abandonment he would have been sworn at'. John defied every man, seeming to challenge his   25
whole world single-handed. For six years he brushed aside the denunciations of the great Pope Innocent III, gathering the Church in England into his fierce hands and squeezing out of it all opposition and nearly all life. 'He feared not God, nor respected men.'   30

[B] The violent temper of the Angevins, their vicious reaction to being thwarted, was almost pathological in its intensity. A misplaced word of praise for the king's enemy, William the Lion of Scotland, threw Henry II into a fit of rage one morning in which he fell screaming out of bed, tore up his coverlet, and threshed   5
around the floor cramming his mouth with the stuffing of his mattress. Frequently he would chew the rushes of the floor in his fury. Richard, believing that he had got the worst of a bargain on one occasion, flew into a blind rage, like a wounded boar, it is said, and no one dared come near him. The chronicler Richard   10
of Devizes remembered John as a young prince breaking out in frustrated fury at Chancellor Longchamp: 'His whole person became so changed as to be hardly recognizable. Rage contorted his brow, his burning eyes glittered, bluish spots discoloured the pink of his cheeks, and I know not what would have become of the   15
chancellor if in that moment of frenzy he had fallen like an apple into his hands as they sawed the air.'

[C] 'From the Devil they came,' growled St. Bernard, 'and to the Devil they will return.' There were many who agreed with him. Popular gossip told of their descent from a devilish ancestress— it was a convenient explanation of their demonic energy, their ferocious ruthlessness. In the days of long ago, when all fairy   5
stories are credible, a certain count of Anjou returned from a distant journey with a strange woman whom he married. She was evidently a lady and very beautiful, but there was much that was odd about her: she had no relatives or friends, she seldom went to church, and when she did always made some excuse to leave   10
before the Consecration. In time her husband became so puzzled by this behaviour that he instructed four of his knights to stay close by her when next she entered the church, and prevent her slipping out. Just as the Consecration was beginning she made as if to leave, but the knights trod on the hem of her robe to detain her.   15
As the priest raised the Host above his head she uttered a scream, wrenched apart the fastening of her cloak to escape from it, and still shrieking flew out of the window. She was Melusine, daughter of Satan, and no evil spirit, as is well known, can look upon the Body of Christ. In her flight she dragged two of her children with   20
her; but two remained and from them were descended the Angevin kings of England. Henry II's sons, with characteristically profane humour, were prone to joke about the story, and to people who protested against their fighting among themselves they

replied: 'Do not deprive us of our heritage; we cannot help 25
acting like devils.'

w. l. warren, *King John* (Eyre and Spottiswoode)

After reading each of the following questions, choose the ONE correct
answer, and indicate it by writing down the letter that stands for it. In all
questions only ONE answer is correct. This is stressed in some questions, but
remember that the rule applies to all of them.

From Section A

1 The first two paragraphs suggest that the author's attitude to the
Angevins

    A stresses their faults more than their virtues
    B idolizes them and turns them into heroes
    C emphasizes their colourful qualities, good and bad
    D illustrates how out-of-date was their idea of kingship
    E makes clear how selfish and greedy they were

2 'Dynamic' (l. 5) means

    A competent
    B energetic
    C impressive
    D irascible
    E efficient

3 'Prejudiced' (l. 7) means

    A misrepresented
    B complicated
    C wrecked
    D contradicted
    E impaired

4 Considering the author's general view of the Angevins one is surprised to read of their

    A 'vast resources' (l. 11)
    B 'clever minds' (l. 5)
    C 'calculated schemes' (l. 7)
    D 'zest for war' (l. 20)
    E 'ruthless energy' (l. 21)

5 'Conceived' (l. 10) means

    A planned
    B intended
    C created
    D prepared
    E modified

6 Which ONE of the following points about these three kings is *not* made by the passage?

A Richard I was the most chivalrous in war
B Henry II had great physical stamina
C John I was the least God-fearing of the three
D they seemed as unusual to their contemporaries as they now do to us
E they were too impetuous to be successful kings

7 Which of the following phrases convey adverse criticism of these kings?

   i 'strong wills' (l. 6)
   ii 'hot temper' (l. 6)
   iii 'human chariot' (l. 12)
   iv 'from dawn until sunset' (l. 16)
   v 'fierce hands' (l. 28)

Which ONE of the following gives the correct phrases?

A i and ii
B ii and iv
C ii, iii and iv
D iii, iv and v
E ii and v

8 'Brushed aside' (l. 26) means

A cancelled
B abolished
C eluded
D ignored
E abrogated

From Section B

9 The strongest word in condemnation of the Angevins is

A 'violent' (l. 1)
B 'temper' (l. 1)
C 'pathological' (l. 2)
D 'intensity' (l. 2)
E 'frenzy' (l. 16)

10 Which of the following can be said of Section B?

   i it concentrates more on the Angevin rages
   ii it states its main theme in its first sentence, the topic sentence, then gives examples
   iii it develops the theme that begins towards the end of the previous paragraph
   iv it is very similar in structure to the previous paragraph
   v in describing Henry II, Richard I and John it stresses their similarities rather than their differences

Which ONE of the following gives the correct statements?

A i, ii and iii
B i, iii and v
C i, ii, iii and iv
D i, iii, iv and v
E all of them

11 'Thwarted' (l. 2) means

  A opposed
  B victimized
  C criticized
  D fooled
  E ridiculed

12 'Misplaced' (l. 2) means

  A generous
  B ill-timed
  C unsympathetic
  D inappropriate
  E insincere

13 Which ONE of the following words is used literally, *not* metaphorically?

  A 'vicious' (l. 1)
  B 'threshed' (l. 5)
  C 'blind' (l. 9)
  D 'glittered' (l. 14)
  E 'sawed' (l. 17)

From Section C

14 Which of the following points are illustrated in Section C?

    i they were cool enough to laugh at themselves
    ii they wanted to shock and frighten other people
    iii their violent tempers were well known
    iv they were as superstitious as the people of their age
    v there was a strong family likeness

Which ONE of the following gives the correct points?

  A i, ii, iii and iv
  B i, iii, iv and v
  C i, ii, iv and v
  D i, ii, iii and v
  E all of them

15 'Popular' (l. 3) means

   A enjoyed by many
   B liked by many
   C believed by many
   D passed on by many
   E credited by their supporters

16 'Ruthlessness' (l. 5) means

   A irritability
   B pitilessness
   C self-conceit
   D greed
   E cruelty

17 'Characteristically' (l. 22) means

   A essentially
   B intrinsically
   C consistently
   D typically
   E eccentrically

18 'Profane' (l. 23) means

   A irreverent
   B atheistic
   C vulgar
   D abusive
   E pagan

19 Which ONE of the following statements about punctuation is *not* true?

   A the dash in l. 3 could be replaced by a semi-colon
   B the commas in ll. 5–6 could be replaced by two dashes
   C the colon in l. 9 introduces a list
   D a comma could equally well have been included after 'beginning' in l. 14.
   E a comma could have been inserted for emphasis after 'them' in l. 21

20 'Heritage' (l. 25) refers to inherited

   A lands
   B money
   C characteristics
   D curse
   E reputation

From the Whole Passage

21 A suitable title for the passage would be

    A Angevin tempers

    B King John and his family

    C The fury of hell

    D Descendants of the devil

    E They feared not God!

22 The author mentions the Angevins' faults and abilities but he

    A becomes more critical as the passage goes on

    B thinks John slightly worse than the others

    C quotes their enemies but not their admirers

    D regards the story as colourful but uninformative

    E partly admires them because they were not deterred from their purpose by opposition or gossip

Additional Question

[*Time allowed: 30 minutes*]

24 a Explain in your own words which qualities of the Angevin kings made them effective rulers.

    b Why was this historian justified in including the mythical story of Melusine in a serious, modern history book?

    c Describe the differences between the interests and characters of Henry II, Richard I and John.

Paper 14

Part One

[*Time allowed: 1 hour for question 1; 30 minutes for question 2*]

1 Write a composition on *one* of the following subjects:

a 'There is no point in work
Unless it absorbs you
Like an absorbing game.'

b To what extent are we slaves of fashion?

c Careers (or one career) that I should *not* like to follow.

d After the rain.

e Two well-known people whose qualities you admire. Say something about their careers and achievements and be precise about the qualities you admire in them.

f Your latest twelve months in school. Write as you wish, but you might like to say something about your friends, your share in the life of the school, your work, events in the life of the school, development of hobbies and social life outside school, the ways in which you have changed during this period.

g A lucky escape. (In telling this story, do not start too early in the story, or spend too much time on the preliminaries that brought you into danger.)

2 *Either*

a Write a letter to the editor of your local newspaper (not to the manager of your local bus company) protesting against the unsatisfactory nature of the local bus services. Invent suitable names and addresses.

Or

b Write an account, of about one and a half pages, of a day in the life of a schoolboy (or schoolgirl) in AD 2000. You may imagine such changes as greatly increased use of television and teaching machines.

Part Two

[*Time allowed: 35 minutes*]

Read the following article (which for your convenience has been divided into two sections) and then answer the questions.

[A] Now that it has more central heating and fewer mouldering gibbets, the countryside is more pleasant than it was. But it is still agreeable to get back to town after a country Christmas, simply because so many people in the country seem positively to detest the times we live in. The seventies to them mean nothing   5
but pylons and noise and overcrowding, tradespeople failing to call and charwomen being wasted in factories; the country is going to the dogs, and even the dogs aren't what they were.

It is an attitude ably summed up by the headmaster of Harrow, I am told, when he looked out of his train window between   10
Slough and London, shuddered, and said: 'Not our century, is it?' I must say it is very much mine, and maybe the New Year is as good a time as any to stand up for it.

We may as well start the argument in the usual place—with those technical and scientific achievements usually dismissed in   15
one scornful half-sentence about moon rockets and electric shoe polishers. But I think one should spare a better word for them.

Modern medicine I am not inclined to pooh-pooh, having survived acute appendicitis; and I cannot help wondering whether the people who long for the peace and poetry of the   20
eighteenth century have considered what dying in childbirth without anaesthetics must have been like.

A good many of the shots commonly aimed at the seventies seem to me simply wide of the mark. Violence, for example. Nowadays, it is true, the youths have the transport to carry their   25
brawls into nice neighbourhoods; but you get a lot less razor-fighting in the Gorbals. Noise—but can anything have been noisier than iron hooves on cobbles? Again, we are supposed to have substituted telly-goggling for the home arts, but to my mind it is not the people who used to go in for part-songs and barbola   30
work who now stare blankly at the T.V. but those who used to stare blankly at the wallpaper.

Youth is supposed to be bored and aimless; yet the figures for every hobby you can name are on the increase, and any of the young that one meets seem to be full of confidence. But even if all   35
these things were true, I am still not sure it would not be out-

weighed by the vast increase in the freedom of choice enjoyed by
working people, young people and, above all, women.

[B] You hear people asking at dinner parties what real benefits the
liberation of women has, after all, brought.

But people often forget that the biggest advance is in women's
legal strength as women—freedom to hang on to their own
children, for example, or to have some sort of legal share in a   5
disbanded home.

It is women, too, who have mainly benefited from the let-up in
family tyranny. I know a woman, now dead, who spent her whole
life as a dependent spinster because her Congregationalist father
refused to let her marry her beloved Anglican. Beatrix Potter's   10
parents were still balking at her choice of mate when she was
forty, and Florence Nightingale wasted fifteen years picking up
her mother's hairpins in the cause of family duty. It was she, too,
who coined the phrase 'busy idleness' for the genteel boredom
that went with the 'age of leisure'. That the servants were down-   15
trodden we all accept, but a lady's existence must have been
restricted too.

And it is worth pointing out that for all the high proportion of
failures, our ideal of marriage must be one of the highest the
world has ever known. The notion of a complete sharing at every   20
level; of fathers taking as much interest in the children's upbringing as mothers, of mothers really understanding a man's
working life: this can hardly have been possible when the man's
world and the woman's world were so separate. We talk about
problems of communication; but a hundred years ago people   25
operated in such separate grooves that they didn't have to
communicate.

The most serious charge against the time, I suppose, is the
decline in morals. But even here there may be something on the
credit side.   30

There is another dimension to morality since the growth of
socialism: nobody now supposes that you can be a good Christian
slumming in ermine and pearls. The most horrifying thing about
Cecil Woodham Smith's book about the Irish famine (*The Great
Hunger*), it seems to me, was not the sufferings of the starving or   35
even the callousness of the evicting landlords, but the fact
that no one seemed to think the famine their responsibility.
Whatever disasters happen nowadays, we do assume that
somebody ought to do something; that at any rate it is our

business. I don't think you can rate our morals without consider- 40
ing the increase in the social conscience, which is the bit this
century has added to the available ideology.

In the regrettable absence of a time machine, it may seem futile
to ask whether these are good times to live in at all. But the point
is that the things that are badly wrong with our times—the 45
ugliness, the remaining social injustice—are not to be put right
by nostalgically looking back to a golden age that never was.
Social justice is not to be had by deploring the Welfare State as a
piece of modern nonsense, but by repairing the holes in its fabric.
It is not the preservation of rural England, but more exciting 50
suburban architecture which is going to make the place look
better.

The Royal Dukes may be as rich as Clore, but they can no
longer command a policeman to arrest me. Widows' pensions
are not what they might be—but at least the poor don't receive 55
the scraps of Blenheim Palace mixed indiscriminately like
pigswill, as they did till an American put a stop to it. We may not
have the serene certainty that God is on the side of the British
Empire—but at least He isn't on the side of father, either.

KATHARINE WHITEHORN, *The Observer Foreign News Service*

After reading each of the following questions, choose the ONE correct
answer, and indicate it by writing down the letter that stands for it. In all
questions only ONE answer is correct. This is stressed in some questions, but
remember that the rule applies to all of them.

From Section A

1 The author of this article believes that many country people
   A complain about too few things
   B have only recently outgrown an attitude that hanged men for
     petty crimes
   C are ingenuously thrilled by recent inventions
   D overrate the value of journeys to the moon
   E are justified in emphasizing the ugliness of pylons

2 The views expressed in the sentence beginning 'The seventies' (l. A. 5)
   are views which the writer
   A considers rather eccentric
   B is surprised to find in her friends
   C exaggerates in order to ridicule
   D is beginning to sympathize with
   E considers inconsistent with one another

3 'Dismissed' (l. A. 15) means

    A ignored and forgotten

    B ridiculed and sneered at

    C driven from one's thoughts

    D omitted from one's arguments

    E considered irrelevant

4 To 'spare a better word for them' (l. A. 17) means to

    A express them more eloquently

    B find politer phrases for them

    C remember them more often

    D welcome them more warmly

    E praise them more fully

5 The writer believes that today

    A violence has grown more frequent

    B young people are easily bored and lack a clear aim in life

    C working people have less genuine independence

    D most people are too fond of television

    E the status of women has improved decisively

From Section B

6 The writer welcomes many changes but does *not* claim that modern life gives women

    A more chance of gaining from a legal dispute

    B more chance to disobey their fathers

    C an opportunity to prove morality unimportant

    D more variety of interesting activity

    E a much closer sharing of ideas with their husbands

7 Which ONE of the following remarks about punctuation is *not* true?

    A the dash in l. 4 introduces two examples that illustrate a previous point

    B it is unusual in ll. 20–3 to separate 'the notion' from its verb, 'can hardly have been possible', by both a semi-colon and a colon

    C in l. 25 the semi-colon sharpens the contrast between the two halves of the sentence

    D the colon in l. 32 indicates that we are about to read what the previous half-sentence has led us to expect

    E the dash in l. 45 introduces a long list of things that are badly wrong

8 Marriages today

    A produce more failures than ever before

    B aim at a truer union of man and wife than ever before

    C leave too many children to be looked after by their fathers

D are based on an unrealistic ideal

E still keep the man's world and the woman's world separate

9 'Balking at' (l. 11) means

    A criticizing

    B ignoring

    C being shocked by

    D protesting against

    E refusing to accept

10 'Let-up in family tyranny' (ll. 7–8) means that

    A the excessive power of parents has been reduced

    B family loyalties have become weaker

    C family traditions have become more flexible

    D fathers can no longer tell their children whom they must marry

    E the persuasive power of other members of the family has declined

11 'A lady's existence must have been restricted too' (ll. 16–17) means that

    A all women were compelled to obey the whims of their parents

    B it was harder for women to rise to a higher class than for men to do so

    C rich women were not allowed to take up interesting jobs

    D women felt imprisoned in their kitchen

    E even the wives of rich men were hampered by a strict moral code

12 Which ONE of the following words is used literally, *not* metaphorically?

    A 'advance' (l. 3)

    B 'hang on to' (l. 4)

    C 'benefited' (l. 7)

    D 'grooves' (l. 26)

    E 'credit' (l. 30)

13 The writer believes that most people today

    A think the community should do more for the poor

    B expect somebody else, not themselves, to avert great tragedies

    C ignore their responsibility for other members of our society

    D have become insensitive to other people's misfortunes

    E are right to stress the disadvantages of the Welfare State

From the Whole Passage

14 The writer also regrets that modern society has *not* achieved

    A a real improvement in the attitude of the rich to the poor

    B greater independence for women

    C more legal rights and career openings for women

    D a firm resolve to improve the architecture of our suburbs

    E increased freedom from arbitrary arrest

15 A suitable title for this article would be

   A God made the country, and man made the town
   B The growth of a social conscience
   C A fine time to be alive
   D The emancipation of women
   E Have our morals declined?

16 Violence, noise and boredom in modern life are

   A very seriously exaggerated by many people
   B decisively different from their counterparts in other ages
   C less significant than the growth of real freedom
   D among its dominant and typical features
   E more characteristic of the young than of the old

Additional Question
[*Time allowed: 1 hour*]

17 a What accusations does the writer make, directly or indirectly, against the countryside and country people?
   b What seem to her to be the advantages of being alive today (rather than in the past) for women?
   c What other advantages are there in being alive today (advantages shared by both sexes)?
   d Explain very briefly the writer's main accusations against the past.
   e Explain the meaning of:
     'dismissed' (l. A. 15);   'liberation' (l. B. 2);   'let-up' (l. B. 7);
     'balking at' (l. B. 11); 'ideology' (l. B. 42).
   f What effects does the writer achieve by using the following words: 'shots' (l. A. 23);   'genteel' (l. B. 14); 'restricted' (l. B. 17); 'grooves' (l. B. 26).
   g Explain fully the sentence: '*We . . . . communicate*' (ll. B. 24–6). What sort of *communication* is she thinking of?
   h Comment on two phrases which are misleading because the writer is unconsciously thinking only of the rich.
   i Comment on two arguments which the writer mentions, but does not believe. How does her choice of words reveal that she does not really believe these arguments when she puts them forward?
   j Explain the writer's views on television.
   k Write a brief letter to the newspaper in which this article appeared, agreeing or disagreeing with one aspect of it.

Paper 15

Part One

[*Time allowed: 1 hour*]

Write a composition on *one* of the following subjects:

a Hallowe'en and twelve of the clock.

b To travel hopefully is better than to arrive.

c Describe a real or imaginary rescue of a pet animal.

d Do you think that prefect systems are useful and suitable in schools today? Suggest some advantages and disadvantages of selected pupils holding positions of authority.

e 'Age shall not weary, nor the years condemn.
At the going down of the sun and in the morning
We will remember them.'
What are your views of Remembrance Sunday, and the ceremonies and practices connected with it?

f Unofficial strikes.

g Write a story, a description or an essay suggested by any *one* of the illustrations on the previous page or on the two following pages. (Your composition may be directly about the subject of the illustration, or may take only some suggestions from it, but there must be some clear connection between the illustration and the composition.)

Part Two

[*Time allowed: 1 hour*]

Read the following article (which for your convenience has been divided into three sections) and then answer the questions.

[A] Why make a film about Ned Kelly? More ingenious crimes than those committed by the reckless Australian bandit are reported every day. What is there in Ned Kelly to justify dragging the mesmeric Mick Jagger so far into the Australian bush and away from his natural haunts? The answer is that the film-makers know we always fall for a bandit, and Jagger is set to do   5

for bold Ned Kelly what Brando once did for the arrogant
Emiliano Zapata.

A bandit inhabits a special realm of legend where his deeds are
embroidered by others; where his death rather than his life is   10
considered beyond belief; where the men who bring him to
'justice' are afflicted with doubts about their role.

The bandits had a role to play as definite as that of the authorities which condemned them. These were men in conflict with
authority, and, in the absence of strong law or the idea of loyal   15
opposition, they took to the hills. Even there, however, many of
them obeyed certain unwritten rules.

These robbers, who claimed to be something more than mere
thieves, had in common, firstly, a sense of loyalty and identity
with the peasants they came from. They didn't steal the peasant's   20
harvest; they did steal the lord's.

And certain characteristics seem to apply to 'social bandits'
whether they were in China, Sicily or Peru. They were generally
young men under the age of marriage, predictably the best age for
dissidence. Some were simply the surplus male population who   25
had to look for another source of income; others were runaway
serfs or ex-soldiers; a minority, though the most interesting, were
outstanding men who were unwilling to accept the meek and
passive role of peasant.

They usually operated in bands between ten and twenty   30
strong and relied for survival on difficult terrain and bad transport. And bandits prospered best where authority was merely
local—over the next hill and they were free. Unlike the general
run of peasantry they had a taste for flamboyant dress and
gesture; but they usually shared the peasants' religious beliefs and   35
superstitions.

The first sign of a man caught up in the Robin Hood syndrome
was when he started out, forced into outlawry as a victim of injustice; and when he then set out to 'right wrongs', first his own
and then other people's. The classic bandit then 'takes from the   40
rich and gives to the poor' in conformity with his own sense of
social injustice; he never kills except in self-defence or justifiable
revenge; he stays within his community and even returns to it if
he can to take up an honourable place; his people admire and
help to protect him; he dies through the treason or perfidy of one   45
of them; he behaves as if invisible and invulnerable; he is a
'loyalist', never the enemy of the king but only of the local
oppressors.

None of the bandits lived up fully to this image of the 'noble robber' and for many the claim of larger motives was often a   50 delusion.

[B] Yet amazingly, many of these violent men did behave at least half the time in accordance with this idealist pattern. Pancho Villa in Mexico and Salvatore Giuliano in Sicily began their careers harshly victimized. Many of their charitable acts became legends. And even the bandits' killing, monotonous in its   5 regularity, may well have been done in accordance with a code too remote to mean very much to us who abhor equally all killing.

Far from being defeated in death, bandits' reputation for invincibility was often strengthened by the manner of their   10 dying. The 'dirty little coward' who shot Jesse James in the back is in every ballad about him, and the implication is that nothing else could have brought Jesse down. Even when the police claim the credit, as they tried to do at first with Giuliano's death, the local people refused to believe it. And not just the bandit's   15 vitality prompts the people to refuse to believe that their hero has died; his death would be in some way the death of hope.

For the traditional 'noble robber' represents an extremely primitive form of social protest, perhaps the most primitive there is. He is an individual who refuses to bend his back, that is all.   20 Most protesters will eventually be bought over and persuaded to come to terms with the official power. That is why the few who do not, or who are believed to have remained uncontaminated, have so great and passionate a burden of admiration and longing laid upon them. They cannot abolish oppression. But they do   25 prove that justice is possible, that poor men need not be humble, helpless and meek.

Some bandits, in fact, went a good deal further than this, and set out to prove that even the poor and weak can be terrible. The vengeance and atrocities of the Brazilian bandit, Lampiao, be-   30 came a matter of pride to local peasants who had generally only been able to identify with the receiving end of cruelty. Such avengers fed the people with a vision of destruction as the only social justice.

[C] Once we come to the greater complexities of modern society, however, its enlarged scope and efficiency, the bandit is deprived

of his power and soon becomes extinct. In modern revolutionary
movements the bandit is often regarded as a doubtful figure
without a useful part to play. Pancho Villa stands out as the   5
great exception, recruited into the Mexican revolution as a
formidable general of their armies.

The bandit in the real world is rooted in peasant society and
when its simple agricultural system is left behind so is he. But the
tales and legends, the books and films continue to appear for an   10
audience that is neither peasant nor bandit. In some ways the
characters and deeds of the great bandits could so readily be the
stuff of grand opera—Don José in 'Carmen' is based on the
Andalusian bandit El Empranillo. But they are perhaps more at
home in folk songs, in popular tales and the ritual dramas of   15
films. When we sit in the darkness of the cinema to watch the bold
deeds of Ned Kelly we are caught up in admiration for their
strong individuality, their simple gesture of protest, their passion
for justice and their confidence that they cannot be beaten. This
sustains us nearly as much as it did the almost hopeless people   20
from whom they sprang.

MAUREEN GREEN, *The Observer Colour Magazine*

After reading each of the following questions, choose the ONE correct
answer, and indicate it by writing down the letter that stands for it. In all
questions only ONE answer is correct. This is stressed in some questions, but
remember that the rule applies to all of them.

From Section A

1 A suitable title for this section would be

  A Why make a film about Ned Kelly?
  B Why we sympathize with bandits
  C The bandits' claim to be Robin Hoods
  D Brave challengers of authority
  E Campaigns against wicked sheriffs

2 The writer of this article uses the colloquial words 'fall for' (l. 6) to
suggest that our sympathy for bandits is

  A justified
  B natural
  C unreal
  D unjustified
  E political

3 Which ONE of the following words is *not* intended to suggest some indirect criticism of bandits?

    A 'bold' (l. 7)
    B 'legend' (l. 9)
    C 'claimed' (l. 18)
    D 'dissidence' (l. 25)
    E 'loyalty' (l. 19)

4 All the following words convey more open criticism of bandits with the ONE EXCEPTION of

    A 'reckless' (l. 2)
    B 'arrogant' (l. 7)
    C 'definite' (l. 13)
    D 'fully' (l. 49)
    E 'delusion' (l. 51)

5 Into which ONE of the following sentences has the writer introduced most exaggeration to suggest that it is not completely true?

    A 'More ingenious crimes than those committed by the reckless Australian bandit are reported every day.' (ll. 1–3)
    B 'The bandits had a role to play as definite as that of the authorities which condemned them.' (ll. 13–14)
    C 'These robbers, ... , had in common, firstly, a sense of loyalty and identity with the peasants they came from.' (ll. 18–20)
    D 'And certain characteristics seem to apply to "social bandits" whether they were in China, Sicily or Peru.' (ll. 22–3)
    E 'He is a "loyalist", never the enemy of the king but only of the local oppressors.' (ll. 46–8)

6 Of the following reasons for becoming bandits the ONE that the writer sympathizes with *least* is that they

    A could not join a legal opposition party
    B tried to help the poor country folk
    C had few careers open to them
    D were unwilling to accept social injustice and inequality
    E liked theatrical clothes and behaviour

7 Which ONE of the following remarks about punctuation is *not* true?

    A the comma before 'and' in l. 6 shows that only the expression 'that the . . . . . . for a bandit' completes the idea commented by 'The answer is . . . . '
    B to use semi-colons in ll. 10 and 11, instead of commas, is not necessary
    C the inverted commas round 'justice' in l. 12 indicate some uncertainty on the writer's part about where real justice lay
    D the clause 'who . . . . thieves' (ll. 18–19) is a defining clause

E '*had*' (l. 26) is in italics in order to stress that the writer really believes this statement

8 'Arrogant' (l. 7) means

    A boastful
    B oppressive
    C self-righteous
    D overbearing
    E cruel

9 'Difficult terrain' (l. 31) means

    A districts where communications were poor
    B times when governments were unpopular
    C land where travel was difficult
    D slopes that were steep
    E circumstances unfavourable to the government

10 'Syndrome' (l. 37) means a concurrent set of

    A legends
    B pretences
    C ideals
    D symptoms
    E compulsions

11 'Classic' (l. 40) means

    A historical
    B defensible
    C typical
    D class-conscious
    E old-fashioned

12 'Perfidy' (l. 45) means

    A weakness
    B cowardice
    C disloyalty
    D desertion
    E malice

13 'Invulnerable' (l. 46) means

    A perfectly justifiable
    B difficult to catch
    C impossible to harm
    D indifferent to danger
    E hidden from authority

From Section B

14 The sentence 'And even . . . . . all killing' (ll. 5–8) means that

   A the bandits were all killed through making the same mistake

   B when bandits killed other people, it was because they obeyed certain rules

   C bandits killed people as a result of a feud or vendetta

   D most bandits were killed only because they began to shock the population as a whole

   E most bandits were killed in horrible ways that repel the modern reader

15 'Began their careers harshly victimized' (ll. 3–4) means

   A received excessive ill-treatment

   B were rapidly punished for their crimes

   C were misunderstood by their parents

   D took to violence through a sense of injustice

   E were led into crime by a corrupting upbringing

16 'Abhor' (l. 7) means

   A condone

   B hate

   C are repelled by

   D fail to understand

   E regret

17 'He is an individual who refuses to bend his back' (l. 20) means that he refuses to

   A repress his selfish overconfidence

   B yield to traditional authority

   C adjust himself to society

   D collaborate with oppressors

   E negotiate a compromise with his superiors

18 Bandits' deaths

   A make the bandits seem less admirable

   B are often caused by cowardly treachery

   C raise the reputation of the police with the local people

   D destroy the legend of bandits' invincibility

   E effectively end a protest movement

19 'His death would be in some way the death of hope' (l. 17) means that when he dies the poor

   A lose all expectation of ending social injustice

   B just cannot believe that he is dead

   C lose faith in the causes he stood for

    D refuse to see the cruel side to his character
    E accept the oppression of an unjust government more tamely

20 'Uncontaminated' (l. 23) means
    A unwilling to commit treachery
    B uncorrupted by bribes
    C refusing to give up their ideals
    D unable to be tempted
    E unchanged by success

21 Lampiao, the Brazilian bandit
    A is clearly stated to have been born into a different class from that of most bandits
    B was less cruel than most other bandits.
    C thrilled the peasants
    D seemed pointlessly vindictive to the writer of this article
    E thought social equality a more important aim than merely punishing the rich

From Section C

22 Modern society
    A helps bandits to survive for a longer time
    B produces revolutionary movements that have little use for bandits
    C prevented Pancho Villa from achieving remarkable success
    D still sustains the bandits' sympathy for the wrongs of modern peasants
    E forces the bandits to operate in towns

23 What makes bandits so suitable as film heroes is that they
    A have a theatrical quality
    B protest against injustice and inequality
    C retain the virtues of a peasant society
    D are sure they are invincible
    E refuse to compromise with the demands of society

Additional Question
[*Time allowed: 45 minutes*]

24 a Using the material in this article, but making it slightly more in favour of bandits than it really is, justify the careers of bandits. Use about 100 words.
    b Comment on three sentences in which the writer states, or implies, some adverse criticism of bandits.
    c Identify, in a few sentences, some of the significant differences that this writer finds between different bandits.

Additional Exercises

Composition Subjects

a Write a letter of application to the personnel manager of a large firm which has a number of vacancies for apprentices or trainees. Include suitable information about yourself and invent names and addresses as necessary.

b Write to a local railway station or coach firm giving details of a school excursion you are organizing and asking for information on a number of points.

c Write to the makers of your record player, tape recorder or electric guitar, pointing out certain defects and asking for prompt action to remedy or replace.

d Write the following letters:
  i Your request to the Area Electricity Board for night storage heaters to be installed in your home. Give full details of your requirements.
  ii The answering letter from the Board making arrangements for the inspection of your house in order that an estimate be made.
  iii Your complaint that the promised visit was not made and asking what will be done about it.
  iv An apology from the Board.

e Write an account of a road accident from the point of view of *one* of the following:
  a policeman; a passenger in a vehicle involved; a newspaper reporter.

f Describe the dress and appearance of two people whom you see regularly.

g Say how illustrations can help a reader to enjoy a book. Refer to two or three books you have read.

h Imagine that one of your friends is missing from a school party visiting a large town. Give details of his appearance which would enable the police to issue a description or to build up an Identikit picture.

i Recommend to a friend (who does not read much) a book which you have recently read. Try to encourage your friend to spend more time reading.

j Describe the school library. Give details of organization and lay-out and explain the system of classification of books.

k Give detailed instructions for *one* of the following:
  i the cleaning and care of an electric or gas cooker
  ii the cleaning and care of a motor-cycle or scooter or bicycle
  iii the making of a piece of furniture
  iv the making of an article of clothing

Interpretation of Statistics

1 Using the following table, describe the results of the introduction of the two-tier letter service.

WHEN POSTED	WHEN DELIVERED						
	% arriving on 1st day after posting		*% arriving on 2nd day after posting*		*% arriving on 3rd day after posting*	*% arriving on 4th or 5th day after posting*
	1st delivery	2nd delivery	1st del.	2nd del.		
First post						
old service	96	1½	2½			
new 5d	92½	6½	1			
new 4d	6	3½	65	14½	10½	½
Midday post						
old service	88	6½	5½			
new 5d	86	12	2			
new 4d	2½	1½	66½	17	12	½
Last post						
old service	53	22	25			
new 5d	40½	40½	19			
new 4d	—	3½	62½	16	16	2

'4d and 5d post March 1969' from *Which?* (Consumers' Association)

2 Study the following notes and table relating to sunglasses, and then answer the questions.

LIGHT   You would probably find sunglasses which let through between 20 and 40 per cent of light most suitable for use in Britain.

As you can see from the table, most of those we tested fell within this range—including many of the very cheap ones.   5

For very bright light, while ski-ing or sailing, you may want glasses that let through less light. There are some of these in the table. And some manufacturers make alternative shades which let through different amounts of light.

ULTRA-VIOLET   A British Standard of Filters for *Protection*   10
Against Intense Sunglare gives limits for ultra-violet radiation. We used the test method laid down in the Standard.

Sunglasses

Key: the more points the better

WITH PLASTIC LENSES

	recommended price £ s d	made in	light let through (per cent)	ultra-violet protection	optical quality	light scatter	frame quality	frame material	weight gm	protection from case
Prova 9010 (British Home Stores)	3 6	Italy	22	●	●	●	▼▼	plastic	29	no case
Unbranded	4 6	unknown	29	●	●	●	▼▼	plastic	29	no case
Prova 9320 (British Home Stores)	5 6	Italy	15	●	●	●	▼	plastic	31	no case
Whitecross 066	5 11	Italy	24	●	●	●	▼	plastic	32	no case
Oliver Goldsmith Luna	1 1 0	France	9	●●●	●●	●●	▼▼	plastic	44	no case
Boots Lightweight Sportsman	1 5 0	UK	19	●●●	●●	●●	▼▼	metal	19	▣
Bartex Men's *Polarising*	1 5 6	USA/Italy	29	●	◆	●	▼▼▼	plastic	31	no case
Polaroid 808 *Polarising*	2 5 0	UK	24	●●●	●●	●●●	▼▼▼	metal	15	▣▣
Correna Super Polarised PL13	2 19 6	France	32	●	●●	●●	▼▼▼	metal	25	▣
Igard Z Ribble	3 3 0	UK	25	●●	●●●	●●●	▼▼▼	plastic	35	no case
Orma Sol-Amor 2429	4 2 6	France	25	●	●●●	●●●	▼▼▼	metal/plastic	26	▣▣
Silhouette 609	5 0 0	Austria	23	●●●	●●●●	●●	▼▼▼	metal/plastic	36	no case
Polaroid 444T *Polarising*	5 5 0	Holland/UK 25		●●●	●●	●●●	▼▼▼	metal	22	▣▣

WITH GLASS LENSES

Product	£ s d	Country	No.	Ratings				▼	Frame	Wt.	Case
Woolworth's Lido with Crookes lenses	2 0	Austria/UK	17	●		●	●	▼	plastic	21	no case
Boots	3 11	Italy	16	●	●	●	●	▼	plastic	38	no case
Bartex	7 11	USA/Italy	24	●●●	●	●●	●●●	▼▼▼	plastic	39	no case
Whitecross 1921	10 6	France	26	●●●	●●	●	●●●	▼▼▼	plastic	45	no case
Boots 115	12 6	Italy	15	●●●	●	●	●●●	▼▼▼	plastic	41	no case
Boots Optically Worked	1 10 0	UK	32	●●●	●●	●●●	●●●	▼▼▼	plastic	38	▣
Pol-Rama G172 *Polarising*	1 19 6	Japan	34	●	●	●	●●●	▼	metal/plastic	48	▣
Wiseman Dubar	2 0 0	UK	19	●●●	●	●	●●●	▼▼▼	metal	31	▣ ▣
Frenchman	3 8 6	UK/France	9	●●●	●●	●●	●●●	▼▼▼	plastic	47	▣
Rayban G F	4 10 6	UK	28	●●●	●●●	●●●	●●●	▼▼▼	metal	37	▣ ▣ ▣
Dennis Searle Model 1	4 10 0	UK	28	●●●	●●●	●	●●	▼▼▼	plastic	52	▣ ▣
Wiseman Solaris	4 15 0	UK	14	●●●	●●●	●●	●●●	▼▼▼	metal	37	▣ ▣ ▣
Zeiss Umbral Sahara	5 15 0	Germany	17	●●●	●●●	●●	●●●	▼▼▼	metal	32	▣
Oliver Goldsmith Goo-Goo	6 6 0	UK	63	●●●	●●●	●	●●●	▼▼▼	plastic	57	▣
Rodenstock Locarno	7 15 0	W Germany	36	●●●	●●●	●●●	●●●	▼▼▼	metal	31	no case
Rodenstock Remo	7 15 0	W Germany	25	●	●●●	●	●●●	▼▼▼	metal/plastic	50	no case
Zeiss Umbral Regent	8 15 0	W Germany	33	●●●	●●●	●●●	●●●	▼▼▼	metal	39	▣ ▣
Metzler Zeiss 752	9 12 6	W Germany	33	●●●	●●●	●●	●●●	▼▼▼	metal	38	▣

Sunglasses given '● ● ●' in the table gave excellent protection. They included all but five of the expensive models, but only a few of the cheap ones.   15

INFRA-RED   As we said, infra-red is not a usual hazard in sunlight. As a matter of interest, we tested the glasses (to the same Standard) and found that five sunglasses cut it down a lot. They were: Frenchman, Dennis Searle Model 1, Rayban G F, Boots Optically Worked and Wiseman Solaris. All these, except   20 Frenchman (which was neutral), had greenish lenses. But a greenish colour in itself does not guarantee good infra-red absorption.

OPTICAL QUALITY   It is no use having a pair of sunglasses which protect your eyes well, if the lenses themselves have   25 faults which may stop you seeing clearly. So we checked for optical quality (see table).

'● ● ●'   means that the lenses were almost perfect.

'● ●'   means that, although there were slight flaws, you would be unlikely to notice them.   30

'●'   means that there were more noticeable imperfections which people might find uncomfortable. But none of the sunglasses we tested could do you any lasting harm.

Related to optical quality is *light scatter* within the lens. When very bad, this fogs your view. Glasses rated '● ● ●' (see table)   35 scattered no light.

Scratches and dirt increase light scatter, so try to keep your lenses clean and unscratched.

FRAMES   We checked that the frames were strong, comfortable and gave proper support for the lenses. We rated them in five   40 groups, from '◀' to '◀ ◀ ◀ ◀ ◀'.

CASES   A case serves two purposes. It protects the glasses from breakages, and the lenses from scratches. Plastic lenses particularly need a case.

None of the cheap sunglasses came with a case. Nearly all the   45 expensive ones had a case of some sort, though only two had a really good one that would protect the glasses if you stood on it. The table gives ratings for all the cases supplied by makers. You can get a good one for a few shillings.

'Sunglasses July 1968' from *Which?* (Consumers' Association)

Questions

a Pick out the sunglasses which are best value for money **i** at less than a £1 **ii** at between £1 and £3 **iii** at over £3.

b Pick out the cheapest sunglasses which are likely to stand up to the roughest treatment when being worn and when not in use.

c Select the pair of glasses which has the highest optical qualities combined with the strongest frames and the best protection when not in use.

d What are your general conclusions about sunglasses with plastic lenses as opposed to sunglasses with glass lenses?

3 Study the following notes and table relating to hair sprays, and then answer the questions.

WEIGHTS and MEASURES   The hair sprays we tested were sold in tinplate cans. These have a built-in disadvantage: you can't see how much you are getting. And unless you know all about ounces, grams and fluid ounces, the information on the label won't help much either.   5

We weighed the hair sprays and found differences of up to 30 per cent in the weight of the contents in cans of exactly the same size.

Get Set, Silky, Spray Net and *Topnote* give relatively little, considering the can size used.   10

We also found one or two underweight samples, but this may · have been because someone had tried them out in the shop. Some manufacturers use seals to prevent this.

We hope soon to report more fully on the problems of aerosol packaging.   15

SPRAY PERFORMANCE   In the table, we have given ratings for spray performance, taking into account both evenness of spray and its pressure.

EVENNESS   You want a hair spray to discharge uniformly so that you can spray your hair evenly.   20

We examined spray pattern in the laboratory by discharging each aerosol at absorbent paper and measuring the wetted area. Most sprays discharged evenly.

Some users found that *Fashion Set, Get Set* and *Top Mark* performed erratically.   25

HAIR SPRAYS

5 = well above average   4 = above average   3 = average
2 = below average   1 = well below average

	price s d	weight g	grams for 1s	smell how mild?	hold	non-stiff	easy to comb?	easy to wash?	gloss and clarity	non-sticky	spray per-formance
Amami	4 7	125	28	1	3	3	3	3	5	3	3
Aqua Net	3 11	113	29	4	4	3	2	3	3	3	3
Baby Doll (Woolworth's)	2 11	84	29	1	1	3	3	3	1	3	1
Bellair	4 8	135	29	3	4	4	3	2	3	3	5
Breck Hair Set Mist	8 8	140	16	5	3	4	5	4	4	3	4
Bristow's Star Spray	6 6	120	18	3	1	3	3	3	4	3	3
Diana Marsh (Mainly Woolworth's)	3 9	127	34	4	2	4	4	3	3	4	3
Dippity-Do	4 11	110	22	4	2	4	5	3	3	4	3
Elnett Satin	9 6	145	15	5	2	5	5	4	5	5	5
Fashion Set (Timothy Whites)	4 6	163	36	1	2	2	2	3	2	2	1
Fields	4 8	162	35	3	3	2	3	3	2	3	2
Get Set	4 7	140	30	3	1	4	3	3	3	4	1
Goddess	5 0	135	27	3	5	2	3	3	3	4	3
Lanalem	4 9	182	38	2	4	1	2	3	1	2	2
Living Curl	11 9	198	17	5	5	3	4	3	4	3	3
My Fair Lady	4 8	140	30	2	3	3	3	3	2	3	3

No 7 Satin (Boots)	7	9	192	25	3	3	3	5	3	3	3	2	4
Outdoor Girl	5	2	150	29	2	4	3	3	3	3	3	3	3
Rainette	4	3	142	33	3	5	2	3	2	2	2	1	2
Rosedale Crystal Clear	4	4	127	29	4	2	3	3	3	1	3	4	3
Satin Set	11	9	198	17	3	4	2	2	3	3	2	2	5
Silky (from Boots)	3	11	142	36	2	2	1	2	3	1	3	1	1
Silvikrin	4	7	120	25	3	2	3	3	3	3	3	3	3
Sof-Set	6	10	135	20	3	5	1	3	3	4	3	3	5
So Soft (British Home Stores)	3	11	227	58	4	3	3	3	4	3	4	4	3
Spray Net	4	7	100	22	3	2	5	5	3	5	3	5	2
Spray 'n Stay	4	7	125	27	5	3	5	4	4	5	4	4	5
Spray Set	8	6	130	16	5	2	5	5	4	4	4	4	4
Stay-Set	3	11	135	34	5	3	4	3	3	2	2	1	2
Sunsilk	5	0	140	28	3	4	2	4	3	3	3	3	4
Supersoft	4	7	133	29	3	3	2	3	4	2	4	3	4
Top Mark	3	11	142	36	3	5	3	1	3	3	2	2	1
Topnote	4	0	140	35	1	1	3	4	3	3	3	2	3
Vitapointe	6	11	175	25	3	4	3	4	3	4	4	4	4
VO5	6	0	130	22	4	3	4	5	3	3	3	5	3
365 (Boots)	5	9	192	33	3	3	4	3	3	3	3	2	3

PRESSURE   If an aerosol sprays too gently it can rain all over you—and get on your skin or clothes. If the spray is too fierce it may be difficult to apply evenly, and it may disturb your set.
A few women found some of the sprays too gentle, but more complained about the aerosols which were too fierce. These were 30 *Baby Doll, Fashion Set, Get Set* and *Silky.*

CLARITY AND GLOSS   Our users were asked to evaluate the sprays they tested for gloss and clarity. Some of them found that *Baby Doll* left their hair a bit dull. *Lanalem, Rosedale Crystal Clear* and *Silky* left a visible film on some people's hair.   35

HOW LONG TO DRY   The laboratory found that most sprays took about six minutes to dry when they were sprayed on to glass plates. Most users found this was fast enough for them.

STICKINESS   The most common complaint about the sprays our members themselves used was that they made their hair get dirty 40 quickly. The stickier a spray is, the more this is likely to happen.
    Our users found that *Rainette, Silky* and *Stay-Set* were more sticky than most others. *Elnett Satin, Spray Net* and *VO5* were among the least sticky.

HOLD-THEORY   Most hair sprays have some indication of the 45 'hold' they give on the label. They usually come as 'firm hold', 'normal (regular) hold' or 'soft hold'—though there are variations on the theme: 'holds your hair firmly but gently'.
    As far as we can judge from our tests on normal hold hair sprays, there is probably a big overlap between these three 50 categories: some normal hold sprays give a relatively firm hold, others give a much softer one.
    Which hold you need depends mostly on your hair and how easy it is to control: in general, our members found that (nominally) firm hold sprays were best for long, straight or greasy hair. 55 Otherwise, the hold depends on the style you want—the more elaborate it is, the more likely you are to want a firm hold spray.
    Remember that up to a point you can control the hold by putting more or less of the stuff on your hair.

HOLD-PRACTICE   We found that many sprays which held hair 60 well had some compensating disadvantage—they made hair stiff, or they were difficult to wash out.
    You can see this borne out if you look at the relevant columns in the table: none of the sprays received top marks both for hold *and* for not being stiff.   65

We suggest you get the softest hold hair spray you can get away with for your type and style of hair: it will probably leave your hair looking—and feeling—more natural than a firmer one.

HOW EASY TO WASH OUT?   You could wash many of the sprays out of your hair quite easily—using water alone. *Bellair* and   70
Rainette tended to be more difficult to wash out than others. The manufacturers tell us that *Rainette* should now be easier.

STIFFNESS   Our users found that *Elnett*, *Spray Set*, *Spray Net* and *Spray 'n Stay* left hair fairly soft. *Lanalem*, *Sof-Set* and *Silky* made their hair a bit stiffer than other sprays.   75

DID THEY FLAKE?   Very few of the sprays flaked off hair. *Spray Set* was marginally the best of a good batch, which included *Spray 'n Stay* and *Vitapointe*. Some users found that *Lanalem*, *My Fair Lady* and *Satin Set* flaked slightly.

HOW EASY TO COMB?   *Breck Hair Set Mist*, *Dippity-Do*, *Elnett*,   80
No. 7 Satin, *Spray Net*, *Spray Set* and *VO5* were found by our users to be among the easiest sprays to comb through. *Top Mark* was rated lowest—but it was not particularly bad.

SMELL   You can get normal hold *Supersoft* with '*Perfume No 1*' and '*Perfume No. 2*'. *Spray Set* comes in seven Goya 'fragrances',   85
and there is an unperfumed variety too.

We asked our users what they thought about the smell of the sprays. They seemed to prefer a mild smell. These included *Breck Hair Set Mist*, *Elnett*, *Living Curl*, *Spray 'n Stay* and *Stay-Set* and the unperfumed variety of *Spray Set*. We have rated   90
the mildness—not the quality—of each smell, in the table.

INFLAMMABILITY   Most hair sprays are very inflammable, because of the alcohol solvent. In the laboratory we discharged each spray at a Bunsen burner flame, and found that all would burn—some viciously, producing two-foot flames.   95

You should use hair sprays with great care, and always keep them away from children: this year a small child was killed because he directed a hair spray at a red hot poker.

HAIR SPRAYS AND HEALTH   Very few of our users reported skin irritation—and it was never severe.   100

None, thank goodness, got spray in their eyes. It is very painful and unpleasant if you do. You should wash your eyes immediately with water, or a weak salt solution, if it happens.

'Hair Sprays October 1967' from *Which?* (Consumers' Association)

Questions

a Which hair spray is the best value for money, i.e. gives the best results for the smallest outlay?

b Which is the dearest and least sticky spray?

c Which hair spray combines the best spray performance with the most gloss and clarity, and the mildest smell?

d If your hair is long, straight or greasy, which spray would you choose, keeping in mind that you want the most you can get for your money?

e What problems and dangers are associated with the use of hair sprays?

Answers to Objective Questions

Questions	Papers						
	1	2	3	4	5	6	7
1	A	C	C	B	B	C	C
2	B	E	B	D	A	B	C
3	E	E	D	D	D	D	D
4	B	E	B	D	B	E	C
5	A	D	A	B	B	D	B
6	A	A	C	C	B	E	D
7	C	C	E	B	C	D	A
8	C	C	B	E	A	C	D
9	B	B	B	C	B	D	D
10	B	E	A	C	A	C	A
11	B	A	E	D	A	E	D
12	D	E	C	E	D	D	C
13	D	E	C	D	C	C	B
14	A	E	B	B	C	B	D
15	A	C	A	C	A	D	E
16	E	D	B	B	D	B	D
17	C	B	D	C	B	C	D
18	B	D	C	B	B	B	D
19	D	E		B	A	A	A
20	D	B		D	B	C	C
21				D	C		
22				D			

Answers to Papers 8–15 overleaf.

Questions	\multicolumn{8}{c}{Papers}

Questions	8	9	10	11	12	13	14	15
1	C	D	D	D	A	C	B	B
2	D	D	E	E	B	B	C	D
3	C	C	C	D	C	E	B	E
4	C	A	D	B	D	C	E	C
5	A	C	C	E	E	A	E	E
6	C	C	E	E	E	A	C	E
7	D	B	E	E	A	E	E	D
8	A	B	E	B	D	D	B	D
9	E	A	A	B	B	C	E	C
10	D	E	E	B	A	E	A	D
11	B	D	C	A	A	A	C	C
12	D	B	A	B	B	B	C	C
13	C	A	B	E	C	A	A	C
14	B	A	E	D	B	D	D	B
15	C	D	B	A	B	D	C	D
16	B	E	C	B	D	B	A	B
17	D	D	C	E	D	D		B
18	E	D	C	B	D	A		B
19	E	B	C	B	E	E		A
20	D	C	D	C	B	C		C
21	C		D			A		C
22	E		B			E		B
23			C					A
24			E					
25			A					
26			C					